Supported in Postpartum:
Stories of Rejuvenating Wisdom

M- Muranda
Bower

Supported in Postpartum:
Stories of Rejuvenating Wisdom

Maranda Bower

Published 2019

First Printing: 2019

ISBN 978-1-79479-767-3

Serenity Grows
P.O. Box 3844
Palmer, Alaska 99645

www.SerenityGrows.com

Dedicated to the amazing mothers I serve everyday.

You all light up my world.

Contents

An Introduction

Writing this book has been one of the most challenging endeavors I have ever happened upon. Partly because I wanted this book to convey the entire story of postpartum. Partly because it required me to heal my own story and put down my personal beliefs and judgements about postpartum. It is no easy feat to represent the multitude of experiences we women have; to balance the beauty and the challenges while inspiring and uplifting. After the years it's taken to put this final piece together, I'm beyond grateful to share this work of art with you.

Postpartum, a time I define as the first several years after birth, changes who you are on a cellular level. As one emerges on the other side of pregnancy, she's thrown into a brand-new body and mind. Every bit may feel completely unrecognizable, from the way she looks and feels, to even the thoughts she thinks. Different fears, different ideas about love, and every notion she ever had about parenting becomes uncertain.

In these moments after birth, few women realize they have just been born again and transformed from maiden to mother (no matter how many children she already has). The only recognizable truth is the uncomfortable feeling of change. To live in a long period of transition—to not know who she is—can easily become scary. This is especially true when she doesn't know what's happening to her, while societal expectations and pressures to return to "normal" are constantly pulling and tugging at the hems of motherhood.

This monumental shift in a woman's identity is seldom spoken about. Try researching the word "postpartum," and the most common topic that you'll find is depression. Research "after baby" and you be bombarded with ways to lose weight and "get your body back," as if it were something that had been "taken away" in the first place. Our society has simply failed to understand *why* women are struggling and, as a result, has become terrified of the changes that this sacred period brings. As a matter of fact, little has been done to discover and examine the depths of these changes and how best to support women during this transition. Instead, our society has been focused on making sure women are informed of the difficulties and bringing awareness to related mental disorders.

As the rates of postpartum depression and anxiety rise to epidemic levels, it's become clear that postpartum is one of the most misunderstood phases of a woman's life. Not only are diagnoses of mood disorders soaring; so too are autoimmune diseases that develop after birth. Unfortunately, healthcare providers and researchers focus is centered on how to make the superficial problem go away, rather than address the root cause itself. In my own battle with postpartum depression and anxiety, along with postpartum bi-polar, rage, and an autoimmune disease with subsequent pregnancies, I learned this lesson the hard way. No one could answer my questions as to why this was happening to me. Instead, I was told it was "normal," a word that should never be used to describe a mental health disorder. Commonality does not equate to normalcy. And postpartum should not become the explanation or source of blame.

Postpartum marks a time of a normal biological shift in a woman's body. As a woman moves through the phases of motherhood, her hormones change to support her needs and her baby's. When these biological changes aren't supported and cared for, however, they shift in a way that is less than optimal. And as a consequence, women see and feel the effects in their mood, hair loss, exhaustion, and more. Few postpartum mood disorders are pathological, as our society claims. Instead, they are symptoms of a much larger problem that stems from massive physical, nutritional, mental, and emotional depletion.

When we look at postpartum in this light, several key points arise. First, it becomes clear that many mood disorders can be prevented. Given the right tools and support, most women can navigate this transition easily without encountering major health challenges. When a woman is fully supported and knowledgeable on postpartum, how her body is changing, and how to care for her specific needs, this transition to motherhood becomes welcomed and even (dare I say) enjoyable. The next key point we learn from this monumental mindset shift is that it's never too late to address the root causes of difficulty and fully heal your body on all levels. No matter where you are in your journey, whatever may still be lingering from your initial transition, healing is at your fingertips.

As you read these stories, you may find yourself looking into your own postpartum experience. Maybe you'll be wondering about your own transformation into motherhood and how it's impacted your family. There may be tears as you feel yourself in these women's narratives, describing experiences that connect us all as mothers. There may be grief, joy, guilt, and sheer love bursting through you all at once. This is perfectly normal and should be honored and processed. To take it a step further, journal all that comes to you as you read each woman's story. From this, you will learn more about yourself in postpartum than what you've ever dreamed.

Although I have spent the last decade researching postpartum and supporting women in their own journeys, I was humbly reminded of some very critical truths while compiling all of these stories. We women are incredibly strong and resilient. Our power to give life completely overshadows the rebirth within ourselves, but both are fiercely powerful and should be treated equal in their own right. Our unique skills as women are the very reason we are so interconnected. Although each story touches a distinctive yet profound postpartum truth, each one is so easily relatable between us all. The bond of mothers can never be broken.

Chapter 1: The Essentials

Never forget that the birth of a baby is also the birth of a mother. No matter where you are in your postpartum journey (or if you're still pregnant), take some time to consider each of these healing steps and assess how you can apply them to your life. I use these same steps with my one-on-one clients to bring them powerful, deep transformations while healing their bodies. The way you heal in the years after birth can either shape you or break you, and how your body shifts and adjusts is all up to you.

The steps below will help postpartum mothers ensure strong, healthy postpartum healing, whether you've just given birth or are six years beyond delivery.

The Essential Postpartum Guide

Align With the Sacred Window of Becoming. To create an authentic postpartum experience that meets your body's personal needs, you MUST first understand the postpartum body and how it functions. When you fully grasp the fundamentals of postpartum, you can rise above society's negative beliefs about life after baby and create realistic expectations about postpartum and your post-baby body. By fully understanding how the body functions differently after birth, you also set the necessary foundation to positively transform your postpartum and your health, including your future menopause.

Prioritize Healthy Sleep. Sleep in postpartum is your lifeline to exceptional health. But how do you get the sleep you need with a gorgeous yet demanding newborn? It certainly isn't simply, "sleep when baby sleeps." Most cultures recognize an extended period of "lying in" when a new mother uses the weeks after birth to rest herself back to health. Although that isn't always doable for the modern woman, the concept of taking it easy can be modified to fit personal lifestyles. The key component here is that sleep is the absolute number one priority for the mother, and should remain so for the first year after birth. As easy as it sounds, this one principle can change the entire course of postpartum. It isn't babies who need sleep training—it's the *mothers* who need it most.

Nourish Your Body. The foods you eat in postpartum intensely effect your gut health, which is why many postpartum mamas experience intense gas and bloating, a surge in food sensitivities/allergies, and a significantly increased susceptibility to developing autoimmune diseases. There is also a direct correlation between the foods you eat in postpartum and how depleted your body feels. Due to the lack of enzymes during postpartum (which are necessary to break down the foods you eat), it's critical that a mothers eats foods that are easy to digest and warming to the body. Broths, soups, and stews are postpartum staples full of necessary nutrients. Nourishing herbal teas are also very beneficial during this time, and pack a lot of energy and healing into a single cup.

Find Your Community. To this day, community is a big part of many cultural postpartum practices. Having an entire team of women to cook your meals, draw an herbal bath, and hold your baby while you sleep sounds like a dream. For most modern women, however, it is a dream far from reality. The Community Theory holds true in that a support group can be powerful, but inaccessibility for so many women means that it's necessary to build community through other methods. If you can't gather a support group of women to assist you in postpartum, or find that the support group you set in place fell through, it doesn't need to ruin your postpartum peace. Pick one person who you know you can rely on, outside of your partner (it's their postpartum too). Have your meals and healing therapies, such as an herbal bath, lined up for easy access. Make sure your one support person knows about your wants and desires during this time, and show them how to care for you in a way that you'd like. Note that hiring a postpartum doula may be necessary if you can't find anyone else to assist you.

Understand Your Hormones. Well over 30% of mothers report suffering mood disorders and disruptions, which are a growing epidemic. Most postpartum mood disorders, however, are not pathological—these disruptions are not the problem, but a symptom of a much greater misunderstanding in postpartum. Learn how your hormones work, what shapes them, and how to support them to your benefit so you can be a powerful participant in their delicate dance back to normalcy.

Pay Attention to Your Emotions. As women, we have been trained through the generations to believe that our emotions are bad, and that to be emotional is to be wrong. Nothing is further from the truth. The emotions you possess are a tool. And when you understand the power of listening to and honoring your emotions, you learn to accept their invitation to make changes and live a better life. Trust your emotions and listen to what they are telling you.

Allow Your Relationship to Change. As you grow into the new role that bringing life demands, you may notice the relationship with your partner changes as well. These changes are a normal part of growing into parenthood. Include your partner as much as possible and always keep communication open.

Accept the Physical Realities. Exercise and movement in post-partum can structure your body exactly how you've always wanted, but only if done right. Often, women think that they can build a strong body again by getting back into the gym sooner, but pushing yourself too hard and too fast can actually set your body backwards. The sensitive balance of postpartum exercise begins gradually. Give your body ample time to heal and adjust its liga-ments, joints, and organs back to their proper places. Then start very slowly in implementing walking, light yoga, and stretches. The easier you are on your body in the first year after birth, the stronger foundation you build for taking on more (when you're ready).

Find a New Normal. Pregnancy and postpartum draw you inward to explore and redefine your own new truth. After much surrender and transformation, there comes a time to step into the light and outwardly share your newfound experiences. Sometimes, you must mourn your previous life before you find this new normal.

Use rituals, small routines, and traditions to support you in finding what works best for you.

Dig Deeper into Yourself. Oftentimes, the mothers I work with say that the journey through postpartum brings up the depths of who they are. Birthing a child into the world can shed many layers and masks, exposing you openly to the world. Many cultures believe that postpartum is a gift that brings a woman the closest to God that she will ever experience in her time on Earth. Allow yourself to feel these emotions and release them for your own healing. Running from the big feelings, past experiences and traumas only gives them the ability to haunt you later. Journaling is one of the most effective and powerful tools one can use to set them free.

Chapter 2: Tales of Rejuvenating Wisdom

Breathe It All In

In my husband's culture, postpartum women do not leave their home for 40 days. Their sole responsibility is to care for their newborn, rest, and heal. Other family members cook, clean, and take care of the other children, if there are any. Once the 40 days have passed, the woman and her baby leave the home for a small celebration where the baby is welcomed into the community.

I remember when he first shared this practice with me, I thought he was crazy. How could I stay home for 40 days and not do anything but care for the baby? Who would provide meals? Who would clean our home? How would I finish school? Even though it didn't seem realistic or possible for me to honor that tradition, I told him I would try and do my best.

When my oldest was born, I was in my last semester of graduate school. I remember thinking I would be "back to normal" right after he was born, and I could return to my classes three weeks after his birth. At least, that was my plan.

But once I gave birth and looked into his little eyes, reality quickly set in. I wanted to hold him and soak him in forever. I didn't want to leave to attend class or my internship. I didn't even feel like myself anymore and I wondered how I could reenter the world as a mom.

I ended up having an entire month at home with him before I had to go back to classes and my internship, and it was wonderful. I didn't stay in my home for that month, though. I took my son on walks and even drove to shop for food with him sometimes. While I did my best to honor the postpartum time, looking back it feels like I was rushing to get back to "life."

When I became pregnant for the second time, my husband reminded me about taking the first 40 days for healing and bonding. Since I was already a mom and had been through the postpartum period before, I knew what to expect and how quickly the days passed. I was also more aware of all the emotional and physical shifts my body and being would go through during those first few weeks.

As I laid on the couch one day snuggling my toddler and looking into my newborn son's eyes, I burst into tears. I couldn't believe that the beautiful beings I was looking at had come from me. It was day three postpartum, the day midwives affectionately call "the day of tears". And I now understood why.

With my third, fourth, and fifth babies, I fully embraced the sacred 40 days practice. Friends set up meal trains for me and even took my older children out to play. The mama village really took care of me, and having the extra support also allowed me more freedom to be present with the baby while others stepped in to help with the rest.

Here are some thoughts I shared when my youngest was only a week old:

"Round belly. Thick thighs. Full breasts. I look at the body that housed my fifth baby and I am extremely grateful to it. Nature is amazing. Women are beyond incredible, powerful, and strong.

As of today, I am one week postpartum. This week has been filled with sweat as my hormones regulate, tears of joy and also of sadness, and lots of love from my family. A true roller coaster of emotions.

Our daughter received her name today, and her umbilical stump fell off as if it was perfectly planned. I also noticed her tiny baby feet are starting to get little lines in them.

Time, please slow down.

These days have been magical and also challenging. The children are in love with their little sister, and I've noticed they are seeking attention in new and different ways. Last night, my three-year-old was up until nearly midnight wanting to spend quality time with me, I am sure. We were playing a special game where I was a purple unicorn and she was a pink one. She must really love me because purple is her favorite color.

As my newborn sleeps on my chest, I look at her little face and I can't believe she came from me. There is something so divine about bringing new life to be. Words will never be able to capture the contentment felt in this moment. As I breathe in her newborn scent, all worries fade away.

My home is a mess, but my heart is full and happy. Sometimes, we need to surrender and let the little things go so we can enjoy the big things. The floors will be clean at some point, but my baby will never be this small again.

I'm grateful for tiny reminders to breathe it all in. Life happens one breath at a time, and the time is now.

Sending you love, sister mama. My wish is that you are able to be present during this time of adjustment; fluctuating hormones and moods; tears, blood, and sweat; round body; and most of all...your initiation into motherhood. And here is your friendly reminder, don't hesitate to call on support in any way you need it. Being vulnerable and asking for help when needed makes you strong.

- Sarah Gyampoh

It's Okay to Cry

"You know who cries a lot? Mommy," my son said, so matter-of-fact. He had asked if my husband ever cried, wondering out loud if it was, in fact, okay to cry as a grown man. Then my son followed up with this acknowledgement that mommy cries a lot.

And I'm not sad about it. Because you know what? I do cry a lot. I cry when I am happy. I cry when I'm sad. I cry when I am angry and can't find the words to deal. I cry when I am frustrated that nothing is going my way and I feel out of control. I am a crier. I am not ashamed.

After my youngest was born and I struggled with the chaos of having two kids under two, I cried a lot—out of frustration that I couldn't be in a million places at once, helping them both simultaneously and making everyone happy. I cried because I was always crying. I worried that my crying was negatively affecting the kids. I was stressed thinking that my postpartum depression would screw them up. Until one day, my own words said back at me changed how I looked at it.

One particularly bad day, I tried to take a shower. My daughter screamed and cried from her Pack 'n Play, and my son just was miserable. We were trying to get out of the house to do something fun, and everything was going wrong. I crumbled to the floor, in sobs, when my then two-year-old son came over and sat down next to me, and started to rub my back. He soothed me with words I so often used with him.

"It's okay, Mom. It's okay; I'm here."

And he held me. In that moment, my outlook on the constant stream of tears changed. Instead of "screwing them up," I was teaching them to have empathy, to be compassionate, to understand emotions. In that moment, my son showed me that he understood, all the times when I was comforting, him that he could do it in reverse and comfort me back. What he did that day was more comfort than I needed to stop worrying about all the crying.

Since then, my children have been my biggest inspiration for sharing my emotions. I let them know when I am going to see my therapist, because I want them to know sometimes you need to talk to someone about how you feel. I never hide my tears; crying in front of them is the best way to be open about it, because they give hugs, and tell me it will be okay, and just love me with their whole hearts no matter what is going on.

- Kate Muse

My Vagina, Forever Changed

Listen to your body and don't overdo it.

This is the advice I was given after I birthed my second child. Sure, there were a few more details in there, but that was the overall message. No one defined "overdo" and nobody told me what to look out for when it came to things going awry. It turns out that this was not the best advice—at least not in my case.

Let me back up a bit and tell you about my first postpartum experience. My birth experience with my first was a bit traumatic, ending with a third-degree tear and me wondering if I'd ever have any more kids. I spent the first couple of months scared to do anything. I didn't change my first diaper until my son was two or three weeks old. I spent a lot of time relaxing on the couch in pain and discomfort. I was afraid that my body was never going to feel like mine again. My road to recovery was slow and it took me awhile to bond with my baby.

When he was a year old, I found out that I was pregnant again. After my initial excitement, I found myself worrying about how the birth would go. I didn't know if I could handle a repeat of my first experience. So, I spent my nights reading and researching so that I was better prepared. It worked, and my second birth was much easier. I felt powerful in the hours and days following the birth, which was the exact opposite of how I felt after my first experience.

Listen to your body and don't overdo it.

It was a couple of days after my six-week checkup when my husband and both boys became sick. By Sunday, the baby was admitted to the hospital for trouble breathing and we learned that our cold was actually RSV. I spent Christmas in the hospital with our sick baby while my husband cared for our sick toddler at home. By the time he was released, I was extremely sleep-deprived and sick myself.

At one point during this period of sickness, I lifted our toddler to get him into the hospital and out of the cold. It was in this moment that I caused damage to my vagina without even knowing it. I remember thinking that I shouldn't have lifted him, but it wasn't until a month or two later when I realized exactly why. My body gave me a warning, but only after I'd done more than I should.

A few months later, I learned about pelvic organ prolapse and realized that I was experiencing this very thing. Pelvic organ prolapse is when your organs (the bladder, rectum, and/or uterus) start to fall into the walls of the vagina. Essentially, your vaginal walls are weak and unable to support the organs around them like they once could. It's a bit more complicated than that and varies from person to person.

While reading about pelvic organ prolapse, I started to see restriction after restriction and felt as though my independence had suddenly been snatched from me. Don't lift over 25 pounds. Get your bowels under control. Certain exercises are no longer allowed.

I found myself in a very low place. I worried that I would never be able to be a fun mom. I worried that I'd have to tell my boys "no" simply because my body was different. I worried that I was doing more damage every time I put my toddler to bed in his crib or lifted him into his car seat, which was still rear facing.

I went to the doctor and was referred out to a Pelvic Floor Physical Therapist who introduced me to some exercises that could help. These exercises were helpful, but I found the most help through a supportive group online. Although it took me awhile, I eventually found a group that gave a more positive outlook without all of the restrictions.

The most ironic part? The group focuses on listening to your body, and gives examples of what that means. The women in the group are supportive, positive, and willing to help you troubleshoot whenever possible. Finding a support system, along with time and truly allowing my body to heal, made a world of difference.

I'm now 10 months postpartum and my outlook on life with pelvic organ prolapse has changed drastically. I still have bad days, but most days I'm able to look to the future and what it holds for me as a mom of two boys. I have accepted that my vagina is forever changed.

But you know what else has changed? My heart and the love it holds for these tiny humans I birthed. And that love is what keeps me moving forward on the hard days.

- Pamela Hodges

Becoming

A peaceful and serene labor.

I prepared for six months for this.

A natural mother.

I honed my mothering skills from the age of four, assured by every female around me that I'd be great once it was my turn.

A perfect wife.

Cheers to trying.

We waited for the right time. We wanted for a long time. We laid a foundation for bliss.

Motherhood was to be the most rewarding experience—humbling gratitude, a deep and unfathomable love, and the opportunity to see your partner experience the same.

The start of my journey was none of the above.

No serenity.

No peace.

It didn't come naturally.

No instant, deep love.

Sure as shit not perfect.

Gratitude solely that labor was over.

No bliss to be found.

My son was earth-side for all of one hour before I desired a break.

What had I disillusioned myself with?

My ushering into motherhood was filled with confusion and sadness, self-doubt and shame.

A darkness so terrifying and all-encompassing it brought me to my knees.

I spent many nights questioning what I had done.

What made me think I was qualified for this?

Why am I not happy?

Who am I?

What am I doing?

Why was I entrusted with this perfect creature?

I longed for the days that I didn't know what this darkness felt like.

My therapist said I was grieving my "old life."

Sounded accurate. When will it go away?

Daydreaming of my son being back in my womb.

Longing for just one more week of not knowing.

I longed, in the deepest parts of my soul, to unknow this abyss of sadness and despair.

Of grieving and earth-shattering shame.

I can't unknow.

For the love of everything holy, please someone tell me how to make it go away.

My child shackled me.

My old life of innocent ignorance is gone.

How can I remove myself from this mess?

This was it—rise or die.

The rising felt a whole lot like I was dying.

My perception of self, shattered.

The illusion of control slipping away faster than I could get tears out of my eyes.

The walls I spent my entire life building were crashing down around me.

My unworthiness now exposed to everyone watching this disaster unfold.

My eyes peeled open to see my inadequacies.

My son's crying to serve as a reminder lest I ever forget.

I sat in storms of shame as I raged at my spouse and felt hot anger course through my veins at the sound of my tiny infant's cry.

The outer layers of my being were ripped away, exposing the most vulnerable and raw parts of who I am.

The hurt.

The overwhelming imperfection.

The failure.

The fear.

The wounds I ran from now glaringly obvious and unwilling to be ignored.

There's nothing that could have destroyed me the way that motherhood did.

I was so gravely ill-prepared.

Motherhood has been the most precious gift and the most challenging transformation I have faced.

It brought me back to myself, a person I never gave the opportunity to exist before.

My authentic self, hidden under carefully-crafted layers of protection.

Every layer obliterated in what seemed like seconds somewhere between being pregnant and being at home with a baby.

All of the most destructive thoughts rush to the surface without resistance.

I am unworthy.

I am not enough.

I am ashamed.

I have denied myself.

I am alone.

I shouldn't feel this way.

I am powerless.

I am a failure.

The truth of my becoming is that none of these thoughts were new.

They had been there all along,

My birth and my postpartum experience just served as evidence that my deepest of fears and darkest of thoughts had come to fruition.

A self-fulfilling prophecy, if you will.

Why didn't anyone warn me?

Now I'm here. Why can't anyone seem to help me?

My now-surfacing emotional wounds and crippling despair laughed in the face of Zoloft.

It seems I wasn't the only one unprepared for the metamorphosis.

My midwife.

My doctor.

My doula.

My therapist.

My family.

Even my mama friends who were also struggling. They were just treading water trying not to drown, too.

No one with actionable steps to move through the darkness without getting lost.

No one with actual understanding of the life-altering transformation taking place in every dark corner of my being.

I was not breaking, I was becoming.

My son was the catalyst that inspired me to live fully, to lean into the unknown.

He has inspired me to look my deepest fears straight in the eyes and tell them to fuck right off.

My son did not shackle me; he set me free.

My motherhood didn't need Band-Aid fixes and an "it's okay to feel that way."

Motherhood asks that I claim my story.

Motherhood asks me to find courage.

Motherhood asks me to come into alignment.

Motherhood asks me to have compassion for myself.

Motherhood asks that I strive for progress.

Motherhood asks that I find forgiveness.

Motherhood asks that I shed my shit.

Motherhood offers me an opportunity to heal.

- Paige Delgado

Building a Village

Laughing Gull Chocolates opened its first brick-and-mortar shop in early February. In what has felt like a lifetime since we opened, I have learned a lot about running a business. Over the same time period— which feels like it has happened in the blink of an eye—I watched my daughter transform from a six-month-old baby into a happy-go-lucky toddler, full of personality, emotions, and hugs. And the six and a half months before we opened the shop? It feels like another lifetime. It's funny how time works.

Before our daughter, Alex, was born, my husband and I thought we were prepared. We knew parenthood would be both rewarding and challenging, but the heights of the highs and the depths of the lows? They came as a shock. I won't go into details about how our hearts melted the first time she smiled at us, how I thought my tears might never stop flowing when she didn't nap for days, or when she cried endlessly until she spit up, nursed some more, and then cried again until she spit up, repeating the cycle. There were days when she nursed all day, barely giving me a break to get a drink of water, never mind go to the bathroom. I'll try to restrain myself from describing how perfectly delicious and sweet her first giggle was. Her laughter, as she looks up at me with her bright, loving eyes, has become my favorite sound. I cherish it each time I hear it, wishing I could bottle it up. More than two years later, there are still highs, and there are lows. I continue to learn every day; the only thing I know for certain—the most important thing that I have learned in these past twenty-five months—is that it takes a village.

My daughter's entrance into the world took place over 50 hours, although I only pushed the last hour or so. She was healthy and happy, latched almost immediately, and I had almost forgotten about the two days of painful back labor I endured. We were discharged from the hospital, buckled Alexandra into her car seat, and the three of us drove the three blocks to our house, which was ours for just more week. Two weeks prior to Alex's birth, my husband, Andy, and I closed on a sky-blue Cape Cod on a corner lot on the other side of the city. We had lived in Rochester for less than a year, and had befriended only our real estate agent and my midwife and her husband. We were lonely in this new city, and settling into a new home while launching a brick-and-mortar chocolate shop and navigating new motherhood was, to put it mildly, daunting.

When we moved to Rochester and decided to start a family, I resolved to follow my dream of "saving the world with chocolate." It was a cliché phrase that escaped from my mouth back in college. I said it again and again, and started to believe I could indeed make the world a better place through chocolate. When we moved to Rochester, it made more sense to me to pursue my goal of starting a business instead of looking for a job in my previous career path. In doing so, I reasoned that I could spend more time with my baby in the early years. I left the hospital with a newborn, a commercial lease waiting to be signed, and overwhelming emotions.

When I was first preparing to open the shop a few months before Alex's birth, Andy casually mentioned to me that he thought we might make some friends through Laughing Gull Chocolates.

"Sure," I responded as I dipped the next truffle into the enrobing chocolate. But I didn't really think so. In retrospect, I don't know why. It certainly wasn't why I started the business. Making friends wasn't why I had a baby either.

Two weeks postpartum, apprehensive of my chosen path as a mom and small business owner, I reentered the workforce, dragging Andy and newborn Alex to the kitchen with me. With the two of them in tow, Andy spent time with Alex so that I could enrobe truffles in between ever-so-frequent breastfeeding sessions. This task that would previously have taken one hour took about four hours. Somehow, with Andy's help and my determination, the truffles were finished, boxed, and labeled. Days later, with Alex was snuggled against me in the woven wrap that my mom had sewn, I stood under a tent at our local farmer's market, selling those truffles to afford the rent I was committed to for another month. As it turned out, life was harder with a little one; the silver lining was that she attracted many more customers to my booth.

While I was pregnant, I frequented prenatal yoga classes at a small business down the street from my new home. The studio, called Beautiful Birth Choices, also held weekly "Breastfeeding Cafes" where new moms gathered, each on their own version of a breastfeeding journey. It was there that I first met Karla and her son, Dylan, who was about six weeks younger than Alex. Karla was looking for a job that she could do with her infant son; I was hoping to find a mom who shared my values, could help with my business mission of "saving the world with chocolate," and who would share child-rearing responsibilities with me. Together, we would embrace the age-old adage of raising children as a village. Karla, with Dylan on her hip (or more accurately, in a carrier on her front) started working to prepare the shop for opening in February. We cleaned, designed, created menus, and made chocolate truffles and bark. Often, we switched off tasks. Karla would sing to Alex and Dylan while I completed paperwork for the city or the county; an hour or two later, I would entertain the two infants as Karla worked on the layout of the room and production in the kitchen. In the early days, we worked as much as we could until the babies needed milk, at which point we took a break to prioritize our little ones. Those frequent joint nursing sessions helped to bond us—all of us—in ways I never imagined. We commiserated over lack of sleep, being "touched out," and shared heartfelt moments as we heard our babies' first laughs together, watched them see themselves in the mirror for the first time, or say "mama" and truly look at us. Not only were we building a business, we were becoming close friends, and building our village.

A few months later, I first realized what had happened as Laughing Gull grew. On a Saturday in April, Lorraine from the neighborhood stopped in. She said hi to Andy and Alex, and chatted with me as I prepared her usual order: a salted caramel hot chocolate. In the room next door, there was a group of people hanging out around our newly-expanded play area. Parents, babies, friends. I went back and forth from the kitchen to the customer area, making drinks, giving my baby a kiss, waving or making a silly face at a friend's little one. Allison, who had become a daily customer and friend (and would soon become our third business partner), was visiting with her daughter, Lucy, and sipping on a chai latte while chatting with Karla. I had one order for a Bourbon Cream hot chocolate; another for a mocha (extra hot, I knew) and I walked into the side room to hand Andrea and Patrick their drinks. Before I went back into the kitchen, I sat on the floor next to my daughter. She army crawled her way to my lap, before setting her sights on a toy that looked more entertaining. All around me, I could hear conversations: the newest skill the little ones learned; plans for a barbecue in the spring, assuming it ever planned on arriving; the economics of the trucking industry; the newest update on local politics...I realized, as I listened and smiled at my baby smiling back at me, that we had somehow created a village.

Two years later, my postpartum journey continues to ebb and flow like high water crashing on Lake Ontario's beaches. Karla, Allison and I have created and recreated routines that fit our now-toddlers' schedules. We meet at the shop every morning, and prepare breakfast together. We have added more structure in our weeks, ensuring that each one of us has a "work" day, and each one of us has a day to spend with the kids. Although we work hard and long hours, we make sure that we each have a day off to spend with our own child. We strive to grow our business and have a healthy work/life balance. My postpartum experience hasn't been easy. I don't know that anyone's postpartum experience is, and maybe that is part of what makes it that much more valuable. I am now pregnant with my second child, and anticipating even more challenges as I navigate being a mom of two while growing a small business. There is one major benefit this time around, though. This time, I have my village. I know that the sleep deprivation, the hormones, the cries (my baby's and my own) will all be part of the experience. I also know that my village will still be there, and that can make all the difference.

- Lindsay Tarnoff

14 Years Later

I wasn't prepared for what it would feel like to leave the hospital without my daughter.

I was prepared to be a mom. This was my second child, so I was essentially a professional at this point. But nothing prepared me for the punch-in-the-gut wheelchair ride from my hospital room to the main entrance carrying balloons, flowers and gifts, but without my baby. People passing by smiled at the new mom parade rolling by. I remember them looking around to see the baby. I also remember barely making it through without sobbing. I had asked why they had to wheel me through the hospital like that, without her. Couldn't I just go straight to the NICU? Why did I have to go to the front entrance? Standard L&D discharge procedure, they said. Required for all patients, they said. So, we went.

At 10 weeks pregnant, I learned what it meant to be "Rh sensitized." It meant that during my first pregnancy, blood had somehow been mixed between myself and the baby. My blood type was Rh-negative and my baby's was Rh-positive, so mixing the two made my immune system develop antibodies against the antigens in my baby's blood (despite taking the necessary precaution of having all the proper treatments/shots during pregnancy). This meant that my blood and my daughter's were incompatible—my immune system saw her blood cells as foreign objects.

Throughout this high-risk pregnancy, my baby was monitored very closely—from weekly to daily as time went on—because my antibodies were constantly attacking and destroying her red blood cells and causing her progressive sickness as the pregnancy went on. At 34 weeks, my team of doctors made the decision to deliver early via c-section. We had reached the point where it was safer for the baby to be a preemie in the NICU than to continue the pregnancy in my womb. It was unexpected, quick, and devastating. My baby girl was a six-pound beauty with long black hair, and I only saw her for a few minutes that first day of her life.

The experience of a "fake" hospital departure, a cruel reminder that our birth experience was nothing like what we expected, set off a period of emotional turmoil and depression that is still hard for me to talk about today—even though my preemie is in high school now. Or maybe I was already headed to a dark place because the pregnancy was so hard, and I just blamed that moment in the hospital for being a pivot point. Either way, I have a hard time remembering much of my daughter's first year. When I think about it, I feel sad, immediately drifting to thoughts about everything that went wrong. I first remember the darkness, the trauma, the heartache.

It's been 14 years (and a lot of therapy), and I still need to take a moment to redirect my thoughts and remind myself of all the things that actually went right during that time. It's strange. During that time, I blamed myself. My daughter was so tiny, hooked up to feeding tubes,

IV's, cuffs and monitors, and I assumed the blame. "My body did this. What kind of mother am I?" I now know that my mind went to those irrational thoughts because of the depression, but at the time it seemed like reality. I wasn't able to recognize all the good in our story because I was suffocated by the bad.

I didn't ask for help. I'm not sure I even knew that I needed help, and I'm not sure I had the vocabulary to express what I was going through even if I had known. I didn't talk about it; I didn't know how. Before my daughter's first birthday, her father and I had separated. Looking back, I think it was probably easier for me to run away from him instead of facing my postpartum depression head-on with him. Maybe he would have been able to help; maybe not. I don't know. We eventually divorced but have grown to become great friends, which I'm grateful for. I've since remarried, and we parent together as a team.

During postpartum, I just thought I was sad. And stressed. And emotional because things were so hard. The pregnancy was hard. The delivery was hard. The NICU stay was hard. The period after the baby came home from the NICU was hard. Having two kids at home under the age of three was hard. Having a newborn was hard. I just thought I was struggling because things were difficult and my hormones were a mess. All of those things were true. But it was more than that.

You are never alone in this journey. We are all mothers on a similar path and deserve to go through motherhood hand in hand. When you see a new mother, ask her how she's doing and show an eagerness to truly hear her. Such a simple gesture can change her life forever.

- Nicole Cody

Why I'm Not Trying To "Get My Body Back"

Pregnancy somehow seems to create an "invitation" or odd level of comfort that makes people feel it's acceptable to comment on a woman's body. Usually it's harmless and related to old wives' tales indicating "it must be a girl" or "he's definitely going to have hair," but it sometimes involves comments about losing "baby weight" or the size of a new mother's stomach. These comments are rarely meant to be insulting or make anyone uncomfortable, but they're just not something that is discussed at any other time. So I'm not sure why they're considered acceptable when related to pregnancy.

Everyone's body is different and everyone's goals for their bodies are different. Imposing what we think is best on what someone else should do about the size or shape of their body just makes no sense, especially when the thought is that you need to "get your body back."

Full disclosure: I love working out and did so through both of my pregnancies. I did CrossFit, lifted weights, and ran (more with the first pregnancy because they're only two years apart) because I have loved it for years. I like being healthy and feeling comfortable in my own skin. But the phrase "get your body back" just doesn't feel right to me, for several reasons.

1) You can't.

It's physically impossible. Your body is forever changed by the amazing thing that you did. It will literally never be able to go back to exactly what it was. Pregnancy and birth are natural, but they are impactful. Maybe you can look the same again, but your body will always be changed.

2) It didn't go anywhere.

My body never left me. It didn't belong to someone else. It is, was, and has always been mine. I can't "get it back" because I didn't give it away.

3) There is never any other time that this phrase "get your body back" is used.

If you have surgery, you don't need to get your body back. If you go through puberty, there's still no reason to aim for your previous life. We acknowledge the changes and the differences. You simply work with your body and its current form going forward. Why should pregnancy be any different?

4) Your body needs different things after you've had a baby, especially if you're breastfeeding, had a cesarean, or had other complications.

Your body is working with a new set of rules, and it's not always healthy to go back to exactly what you were doing before you got pregnant. Your hormones are fluctuating, you may not be getting the same amount of sleep, and you're physically recovering, not to mention other individualized issues that you may also be dealing with.

What I am personally looking forward to is being healthy and strong in my body as it is now. I am also looking forward to building that body back up when it is no longer depended on for sustenance by another life. I have been pregnant and/or breastfeeding for almost four years, and am definitely looking forward to not having to think about what goes into my body when and how it is going to affect someone else. I am looking forward to lifting heavy weights again. I am looking forward to wearing clothes that don't necessarily need to be nursing-friendly. I am looking forward to showing my children that it's good to have goals for yourself, and that they should be determined by *you* and what *you* value, not by what other people expect of you.

For me, there is no body that existed "before" this one. It is the same one. And I am just as committed, if not more, to making it the healthiest, strongest, and best it can be—whatever that looks like for me. I wish the same for every postpartum mama.

- Christi Campbell

Having a Baby is Supposed To Be the Happiest Time in Your Life

Today is the tenth anniversary of my realization that I had postpartum depression. I don't call it a "diagnosis." It was a realization that something wasn't right for me, and I could no longer hide it from my friends and family. My baby was almost three months old. It wasn't until over two months later, when my baby was almost six months old, that I was officially diagnosed and began treatment for postpartum depression (PPD). By that time, the PPD had escalated to full-blown postpartum psychosis (PPP).

PPD/PPP is a horrible and debilitating condition. At the time, I was a single mother with a newborn baby boy. I had no support as a new mother, no family nearby, and definitely was not getting enough sleep or nutrients. Ooh, the irony—the doula who had no support!

So hindsight is 20/20, right? Right. I had always had on/off bouts of depression and anxiety throughout my life, but nothing like this. I wasn't planning to have a baby, and definitely wasn't planning to have a baby alone. I had moved from Chicago to New Jersey to finish my nursing degree on the path to midwifery school. I met a great guy...and you know the rest.

My son was born four weeks before his due date. He was born on the morning of moving day. I came home from the hospital with my tiny little baby to an entirely empty apartment. The movers had to re-schedule, and I couldn't stay in my old place with a new baby. Money was tight because I was not entitled to a paid maternity leave. My friends had been the baby's father's friends and family; they stayed his friends and family when we separated. And then the legal actions started. I was treated like a criminal when all I did was have a baby. Was this his way of contesting?

The anxiety, the loneliness, the fears... Everything started to feel totally out of control.

I tried to talk to family and to old friends about my feelings and my thoughts. Nobody understood. When I told them how I felt, those I loved didn't believe that what I was saying was true. Family told me, "Snap out of it!" and, "You wanted a baby, you got a baby." I felt completely alone and uncared for. I had trouble sleeping; I couldn't eat and was losing weight at a rapid pace. I just wanted to run away. The simplest things started to become scary. I had a hard time driving and trusting myself while driving. It was difficult to take care of myself while taking care of my baby. Simple things like preparing a meal were too much effort. Then the OCD set in.

I checked the locks, the stove, the carbon dioxide alarm, smoke detectors, etc. *constantly*. While driving in my car, I needed to pull over to make sure the car seat was in the backseat with the baby in it—that I didn't leave the car seat and the baby in the driveway. I ran out of the shower thinking I could hear the baby crying or that I smelled smoke in my apartment. I didn't trust myself or anyone. I had intrusive thoughts and intrusive visions. I thought that my baby would be better off without me.

I lay in bed at night planning my own suicide. That's not easy to admit, but it's true. I needed help. Back then, I didn't know what I know now, and there wasn't the postpartum support we have today. I wasn't a doula yet, and the awareness of PPD/PPP was not yet prevalent. We still have a long way to go, obviously. Believe me when I say that there were therapists and doctors who told me, "I don't know how to help you." There is better help now, but not by much.

I found a therapist in Manhattan, over an hour's drive from my home, who finally understood a little bit of what I was feeling. He listened. He called me during the difficult times of the day, always early in the morning and in the evening. It took about 18 months to get my life back somewhat. With a lot of patience, the right support, self-care, and medication, I survived postpartum depression, postpartum anxiety, postpartum OCD, and postpartum psychosis.

If you are struggling with postpartum or perinatal mood disorder, or something just doesn't feel right, there *is* help out there. Your family deserves a healthy you! You are not alone. There is help and there is support.

- Nicole Buratti

A Sleepless Transformation

There I was, lying in the hospital bed. Exhausted. Numb. Lost my voice from screaming so hard and for so long. All day of agonizing pain. All of this unimaginable pain; the kind of pain I thought I was not capable of handling. At the end of 30-some hours, a tiny, rather good-looking chunk of life landed on my chest, staring at me. I became a mom. I didn't know whether to be happy, sad, or what. I was still feeling so shaken from taking in so much physical terror. I was told among the dozen or so women who gave birth the same day, I was the smallest mom with the biggest baby.

I never liked babies or kids; I never wanted a child of my own. Children were unpredictable with their outbursts and even harder to keep clean. The sounds of their cries and screams made me internally snap and extremely impatient. Most importantly, I did not want to bring a life into this crazy, violent, unethical, sick, and dangerous world. My loving husband, however, was very persistent in persuading me to at least have one child, and I finally gave in.

When my husband and I were sent to our hospital room with this newborn, we were totally drained from not getting any sleep. We should be asleep, now that the "work" is done, but the tiny little life force wouldn't stop crying. Is he hungry? Is he cold? Is he okay? Thinking about what I could do for him consumed me. Not out of frustration or with the intention of getting him to shut up—it was purely and entirely because of this unfamiliar-but-strangely-familiar sense of unconditional love. Trust me when I say, I am usually very cranky when I go without sleep, and especially without sleep and a baby crying non-stop right next to me. My husband usually is the one who is very calm and loving, but this time it was the opposite. We completely and involuntarily swapped roles, and he was amazed at the way I responded naturally to our son.

When we were released from the hospital, our son, Kian, had to remain in the NICU due to jaundice. Although I knew that it wasn't a big problem, leaving him in the hospital was utterly heartbreaking. We checked on him daily for a few days, and finally brought him home. From the moment we were home as a family, I was on a lockdown. I hired two postpartum nannies (both of them were friends who volunteered to help out for a fee) and they gave me a set of rules:

- Stay in your room and keep the temperature set at 78 degrees.
- Keep your cat out of the room.
- Do not come downstairs.
- Do not open the refrigerator.
- No showers for a few days.
- Do not eat anything other than what we cook you. (In Korea, there are specific postpartum foods for recovery and for production of milk).

- We will bathe your baby.

Sounds a bit obnoxious, right? These were a very standard set of postpartum rules to follow in the Korean culture. It is believed that after giving birth, all of the joints are opened and expanded, so any exposure to cold can make the bones and joints frail and can cause problems later. Another reason why I was not allowed to walk up and down the stairs was to protect my knees from giving out. The postpartum nannies cooked three meals and two snacks for me and my husband; did my laundry, folded it perfectly and put it into the dressers; vacuumed the floors and even the vents; washed the dishes; bathed the little one and kept me company; loved my cat; and even rearranged my furniture, making my home look nicer than ever before.

All I had to do was sleep and nurse my baby. It was nice, and the nannies were the perfect helpers. Even so, I was nursing the baby every 1.5-2 hours all day and night. I can't say I remember ever actually sleeping. I would call it more like a "rest my eyes for a moment and go into a short trance" before immediately snapping awake to the sound of a hunger cry. I was an absolute, undeniable zombie. My boobs were a total slave to this little munchkin, all hot and hard to the point I could literally cook cabbage leaves by laying them on those milk-producing machines. I was a slave to this baby, waking up like clockwork, getting a tiny break when "allowed." I looked so nappy, unkept, living in my pajamas all day every day, still recovering from the physical traumas of giving birth (never knew what a sitz bath was until then), still look-ing so grossly out of shape, that I had all the reasons to hate this whole prison-like experience. After all, I was always an independent, social, outgoing, active, in-shape, well-kept, love-to-do-what-I-want kind of a gal.

But I didn't mind at all. I never once complained or dreaded what I had to do—it just came naturally. I actually really enjoyed nursing; it was the one thing that only I get to do with my son. I was cherishing every single moment. It didn't bother me that I didn't get to sleep much, although I spent the next six months waking up every two hours every night to nurse my baby. Sometimes I didn't even attempt to sleep, knowing that it was pointless since I had to get up anyways soon after. Of course, there were many times when I was frustrated and irritated; after all, my son was an expert at testing my patience. But since becom-ing a mom, my patience has been stretched out. I never thought I'd be this resilient, enduring this many outbursts yet having this much calm-ness.

When we found out our son is speech delayed and had difficulties communicating and learning, I kept his spirits high and encouraged him to be a positive, happy, and resilient kid even when others may be la-beling or judging him. I never told him about these problems or expressed concerns. I knew that you always get what you focus on, and the mind always reflects back on you what you think of yourself, so I decided I was going to be his biggest cheerleader. It wasn't always easy, but he was certainly transforming me into a person with phenomenal coping skills.

I remember that even when I was so tired and so turned off by the weight-gained reflection in the mirror, I couldn't stop staring at my son. When he was awake, asleep, nursing, crying. Every moment was a blissful moment. I even cried tears of joy from the depth of love that I felt came from the very core of my being. I was a new person, a new woman; it was a new life. I felt a true physical and emotional transformation. Every part of my being, every cell, every hormone, every thought pattern—all of me turned into this oxytocin-filled, undeniably selfless, so soft and comforting yet so strong and resilient human being known as a mother. The one thing I thought I never wanted in my life turned out to be the most cherished blessing of my life. I made a promise to myself to become a person that my son would be proud of, that I would be proud of, and who leads by example. Now almost six years later, I am still on that journey to bettering myself and my son. He is my biggest inspiration and motivator, and the one who is raising me to be that person.

We are each other's parent, exploring together; learning, loving and understanding each other as we go; teaching each other life lessons; and embracing this beautiful journey together as a mother and son—as partners, an ever-connected unconditional bundle of love.

- Ara Ko

The First 48 Hours

I remember the moment I felt something within me, a little click in my pelvis. That was the moment I knew little Allie (*name changed*) would come to be. From there it was smooth sailing—a pregnancy without vomiting and with months six through nine perfectly timed during the chill of fall. In my eighth month, preeclampsia became a 'thing' we had to consider, but not a 'big thing.' And then shortly thereafter, one day after a walk and some lunges, labor began during a nap and quickly progressed. A mere four hours later, there was Allie, born at 39 weeks and weighing 4 pounds and 14 ounces. She entered the world naturally, without an ounce of any drugs. We could not have asked for more.

At that moment—4:15 pm on December 13—our postpartum journey began.

The pain, the intense pain. After hours of skin-to-skin, which was an unforgettable experience of baby searching for, reaching and latching just the way a baby should, and much mommy-baby love, Allie was safely in the nursery. She was cradled in the rocking chair by her father, Charlie, who doted on her in the way that only a first-time dad does.

And then there was me, 12 hours later.

Alone.

To rest and recuperate. I needed it, and yet...

The pain would not escape me.

I lay down, I stood up, I held my legs tight, tucked my chin, and curled into the fetal position, trying to comfort myself. Nothing helped. The pain tugged at me, stabbed me in my head and mostly my belly.

Is this normal? No.

But it must be. Yes.

Call for help? No.

Be a drama queen? No, I would not stand for that.

The *pain*.

Unending.

Worse than labor.

Could not be normal.

I swallowed my pride.

I did it—I called the nurse.

And then...

She was calm. She came in, took my vitals, and did not seem alarmed. Went out; came back in.

And me.

I could not sleep. I could not walk. I could hardly wriggle any direction. The pain was eating me. I tried breathing, pretending I was in labor. It would not help.

The nurse came back. Before long there were more. Charlie came too with our little bundle of love. I wanted her back. They told me I'd be alright. They mentioned some terms I'd never heard before, and before long I was whisked away out of Recovery and back to Labor &

Delivery where they needed to monitor me more closely, though I did not know why.

And then amidst the blur of this and that, the doctor mentioned HELLP syndrome. My enlarging liver causing the pain, the risk of hemorrhage, protein in my urine. It was severe. I was at risk. My precious baby was safe. I was a mom.

A choice...bedpan or catheter. I preferred a bedpan. They said catheter. The catheter went in. That was degrading. Ugh.

As the pain subsided, the magnesium sulfate* blur quickly set in.

In my foggy consciousness over the next 24 hours, I remember so distinctly a moment of nursing little Allie. Lying on my left side, dozing in and out of sleep, her lips gently suckling and me holding her close. Those teeny fingers, microscopic toes. Bliss in all the chaos.

Why? Why was this happening? Why me? And also, why not me? Had I had it too easy?

At the same time, I was completely overcome with gratitude—for making it, for a precious princess, for a natural birth, for a loving family, for treatment, for surviving. Truly.

And the small things made a humongous difference. Like when the head nurse came in to give me a massage, or when a friend showed up with soup that hit the spot, or when my sister gently allayed my fears of breaking my very own baby and taught me how to hold and turn my little bundle from breast to breast.

The catheter came out, and...just like that, the next 12 hours felt so normal. Almost comfortable. I was alive and my baby, though tiny, was doing well.

Six years and four kids later, the many lessons I learned in those first 48 hours postpartum are the most profound. Here are a few:

- Advocate for yourself. You—and only you—know what you need, know how you feel, and have YOUR intuition. Whether in a medical environment or otherwise, stand up for you.
- Be grateful. I've adopted (to be cliché) an 'attitude of gratitude.' The effects are tangible.
- Doing difficult, uncomfortable, and upsetting things (like getting a catheter) are a way of life, and sometimes out of your control, but you're not alone. Just internalize this and know that you are not alone!
- Accept and ask for help. It's okay that you're not able to do everything, and especially not all the time. Accepting help to the extent that I needed to (including having other people care for the baby I had just birthed) during my first 48 hours postpartum was tough, and not something I anticipated. Since then, I've been working hard to accept and receive help from others who want to help me. It is a win-win and so important. There is no shame in saying yes; or even more importantly, in asking for help when you need it.

So, to all you mamas out there in the thick of postpartum, or about to embark on your postpartum journey, go easy on yourself. It's imperfect. And whatever it is, however it feels, you've got this!

*In most cases, HELLP is diagnosed before delivery and the treatment is delivering the baby, sometimes quite premature. I was lucky that I had already delivered a healthy baby before HELLP became an issue, which left me at risk but not my baby. In cases like mine, hours of treatment with magnesium sulfate—which leaves one in a cloudy fog for the duration—is common.

- Jodi Fried

The Best Decision I've Ever Made

Postpartum was hard.

When I first thought about having a baby, postpartum wasn't on my mind at all. I was just excited to have a brand-new baby that I could call mine.

Unfortunately, postpartum wasn't all sunshine and rainbows. It was a complete shock!

I was still fat, my lady parts hurt, I couldn't sit, I couldn't poop, and I definitely wasn't having a romantic life. On top of trying to heal myself, I was now in charge of a little person who couldn't do a single thing for themselves.

It's exhausting.

I went through a string of emotions because now I was adjusting to this new mommy life and dealing with raging hormones.

If I could skip the postpartum all together, I would.

A large percentage of women deal with postpartum depression and anxiety every year, and I was one of them. I joined the club.

On top of that, my daughter was colicky. Those don't make for a good combination, so, needless to say, I was hating life.

I hated my daughter, I hated being a mom, and all I felt was regret.

I couldn't bond with my daughter, and I didn't want to be around her.

I felt hopeless most of the time, and all the joy had been sucked from my life.

I felt like I could deal with all the physical aspects of postpartum—and even the sleepless nights—but the emotional burden was just too much for me.

I had reached a new low, and I didn't know what to do. I acted like everything was okay for my friends and the outside world, but on the inside I was drowning.

I was about to burst at the seams one day, and when my husband came home I just laid it all on the table. I told him everything and anything that was on my mind. I didn't filter *a thing*!

He said, "We need to get you some help."

So...I got help. That was the best decision I have ever made, and I wish I would have done it sooner.

Getting the proper help, through therapy and medications, gave me the courage to speak out to friends and family who supported me completely. Because of that, I was also able to bring up my struggles in my casual relationships.

Turns out, more moms struggle with the adjustment to becoming a mom and motherhood than I had ever realized. This led me to my passion of blogging, and helping other moms adjust to motherhood, and see the joys and struggles of being a mom.

This is my story in a nutshell.

There were too many long, sleepless nights, hours spent on my knees, oceans of tears shed, and lonely days. I could fill a whole book with stories about those days, but then you wouldn't be able to see the good in motherhood.

This time of my life really sucked, for lack of a better word. But I believe that things in life suck for a reason.

Even though I felt hopeless, I also knew that God was with me. He gave me strength on my hardest days, and little tender mercies of hope to keep me going.

My good days now are that much sweeter because I know what the lows could be.

I have learned to be honest about who I am, when I'm having a hard day, and that it's okay to hate being a mom some days. This doesn't mean I love my children any less.

Through my struggles, I've been able to relate to other mothers, and start a blog to reach even more moms.

My daughter and I have been through so much together, and our bond today couldn't be stronger. She just turned six and she is my little mini-me. I couldn't imagine our family without her in it, and when I think about the love I have for her, my heart overflows.

This may not have been the motherhood I imagined, but it's so much better!

I continue going to therapy for my depression and anxiety. I currently don't need to be on any medications because I have created strategies in my life to manage my mental illnesses on my terms.

I still have hard days, but it's so worth it for my sweet babies.

- Charleah Alexander

Healing Through Birth

Out of five births, I have had four rounds of postpartum depression. Childbirth is hard on me. Not the birth itself; I love giving birth...but my body can't deal with the hormonal changes. After the hormonal shift, it doesn't take much for me to go downhill fast. And it can take awhile to get through it.

With our oldest daughter, we had a mainstream hospital birth. We didn't even know there were other options. People around us pushed us in this one direction. I was forced against my will and felt abused by the nurses in the hospital and our gynecologist. Getting through that was hard and terrible. I failed my child, I failed myself, and I knew that the experience wasn't okay. A postpartum depression was inevitable, but eventually I got through.

Our second daughter came 15 months later. We hired a midwife and planned to have a homebirth this time. A do-over. I really wanted to do it right this time. But our daughter came a month early and the midwife sent us to the hospital again. It was a different hospital this time around; one that was known for gentle birthing and allowed our midwife to do the birth instead of their own staff. The birth came suddenly, and I didn't realize what happened until our daughter was a day old already. Even though she was born perfect, life with her wasn't easy. From 10 days old until 19 months old, she was sick all the time. I felt like the birth that should have been perfect was stolen from me, and a new postpartum depression fought its way through the mess on top of the burden of struggling with a sick baby.

Ten months later, I got pregnant again. Unplanned, unexpected, but oh so wanted. I'm extremely fertile and birth control isn't always strong enough to hold off pregnancies, despite our multiple contraceptive methods. But the baby was loved from the start; we would figure it out, and we would manage. I secretly hoped that I would have another chance at my perfect birth too. Our third daughter was born at home one day before her due date. It was a whirlwind delivery. There were 20 minutes between the first signs of labor and her birth. It felt like another birth went by me, this time because it was too fast. I had so many hopes and dreams for this birth, but I wasn't prepared to be done with it in only 20 minutes.

Having three children that close together had its toll. I don't think I truly recovered from my previous postpartum depressions, as there wasn't enough time. So, the depression continued. My husband wasn't the kind of person to look for professional help for me, so in the end it kept lingering, untreated, for three years.

Five years later, life cleared up again and we decided to take another chance on a child. I always dreamt of a big family, and it broke my heart that I would need to give up that dream. We tried again and got pregnant...to have a miscarriage at 12 weeks. Believe me, my faith in life was gone. But again, we got through it and got pregnant again a year later.

That pregnancy was a challenge. I was ill for seven months and started to have Braxton Hicks contractions seven weeks before the due date. I had waves and labor pains for eight weeks, but our first son was born at week 41! His birth was wonderful. At home, unassisted, but with the help of a doula; enough time to be aware that I was giving birth and to actually enjoy the birth itself with candlelight, light music, a waterbirth and a lotus birth to top it off.

One might think that it was perfect and, looking at the birth itself, it was. But my husband started to act out a few hours after birth, fought about every little thing he could fight about, and didn't spare me or my new hormones at all. He sent our other kids away to his parents, because he wanted to sleep and didn't want to deal with them. It didn't matter that I wanted them with me, delighting in our new bundle of joy together. In the end, he stole my entire postpartum, leaving me feeling empty and broken. Another round of depression was the result. He lost his job during that pregnancy, so the birth must have been his trigger to break down. He ended up being scared of the world and leaving me in charge of income and everything else. He took my role of mother and wife of the house and hid himself behind it, making it impossible for me to be a mom to my baby. I fought hard to stop it in time, but the hormonal changes on top of everything else were too much and another postpartum depression was my destiny.

I was done with it all. No more babies! My dream of a big family was shattered, but I wouldn't go through another birth or postpartum period. Forget it! I was done. Never again. Even though we fixed our marriage during the four years after our son, I wasn't willing to try again. The risk of being left with another bad memory was too high. I didn't want to do it anymore.

But a little soul had other plans. Even though I was very careful to not get pregnant, a new baby was on its way four years after his brother. I was so scared! Instead of a postpartum depression, I had my first prenatal depression. I couldn't stop crying the entire pregnancy, scared of what was going to come our way and even more scared that I would mess this baby up too. Every experience from our past rushed back in and anxiety took over. What a pregnancy!

A few days before birth, I was finally ready to have this baby. I hadn't been able to really connect with him yet and was scared that I wouldn't bond with him after birth too, but that fear was unnecessary. Nearly four weeks early, our baby decided that it was time to come and offered me the most perfect birth I could have ever dreamed of. In our cabin in the woods, with all our children around. Our second daughter walked with me through the forest when I was singing through the waves; our third daughter decorated my birth nest and photographed everything; our son was present and made jokes while I was giving birth to lighten up the atmosphere; our oldest daughter caught her baby brother in her arms while I delivered him standing on my two feet.

Everyone knew my fears of having to go through a repeat of my other postpartum experiences, and they all made sure that I had the best one ever. I felt like a queen, with everyone working together to make it happen for me. For the first time, I didn't have a postpartum depression. If anything, this experience gave me strength I didn't know I had within me. It was liberating, empowering and lifesaving. It was perfect.

People don't understand how important it is to have a birth and postpartum period that touches your heart. The whole idea that "the only thing that matters is a healthy baby" is nonsense. It's equally important that a mother can connect with her pregnancy, birth and postpartum period. Interrupting that experience can cause so many hormonal and psychological problems—and it's time that we acknowledge this part of being a mother. I was lucky to have experienced my last birth and postpartum week the way I did. I know it would have broken me if things went wrong again. But instead, the experience lifted me up and made me the strongest version of myself that I have been in the past 15 years! I'm standing straight now, carrying the past as a scar on my heart, but also embraced by a maternal power that I didn't know I had in me. My perfect birth and postpartum period were the biggest blessing ever. I can move on now. My last and perfect birth healed me.

* The term "birth rape" refers to medical procedures or interventions during labor and delivery that occur even after a woman has declined or refused help. It is not a legally-recognized medical or criminal term.

- Katia Smits

How My Plump Postpartum Body Helped Me Learn To Love Myself

Fat, plump, obese, fluffy. Over my lifetime, I have been called all of these and more. I've spent most of my life struggling with body image issues and have painful memories of being called cruel names as a child. Sadly, some of my earliest childhood memories include feeling guilt or shame about my body and food. It was shocking to realize I've spent more of my life than not on a diet or some strict regimen to help shed what I considered excess pounds. When I look back at old pictures before and after pregnancy, I can tell you not only what I weighed, but which diet I was following at the time. Every diet, every daydream of plastic surgery or effortless weight loss was fueled by one thing: wishing my body looked different.

During each of my pregnancies, new struggles with food and body image surfaced. I set limits on how much weight I thought was reasonable to gain. I tried to balance my pregnancy cravings, increased nutritional needs and the nasty habits of restriction from my past. "Maybe I can allow myself to eat more if I exercise," I argued with myself.

Pregnancy is often a time when women become more self-conscious regarding their weight. For some, it's an opportunity to allow themselves some freedom with food choices. For others, pregnancy and the (normal) extra weight that comes with the territory is fraught with even more issues with body image. Some women even despise their bodies during pregnancy—they may feel disgusting, lazy, unattractive...and the list goes on. The fact that their body is nourishing a baby makes no difference—any excess weight is still unsettling.

I was no different. I constantly felt like I needed to gain "only what was necessary" to sustain my pregnancy. The less weight, the better. This ideal was only solidified further when my mother made comments about my size, and how difficult it would be to lose the "baby weight" later. I found myself an even bigger slave to my scale, weighing myself repeatedly throughout the week. I tried to persuade my body to gain less weight in the first trimester because I knew most weight gain was expected during the third, right? Don't gain too much weight too soon or you will really balloon out at the end.

When you have struggled with body issues and disordered eating for decades, it's hard to think differently just because you're pregnant. During my most recent pregnancy, I knew exactly what I weighed every week and my total weight gain the day I went into labor. I also weighed myself after I gave birth and every day for about a week. Those numbers *needed* to go down! And they did for two weeks...then I plateaued.

Then I *gained weight* and found myself in the pit of self-loathing and body hatred once again. I checked my Instagram feed and saw the wave of before-and-after pictures of women pre- and post-baby. Their thin, perky bodies looked perfect nestled against their adorable new-borns. And me? I felt massive, lazy and guilty about my food choices once again. The temptation of restriction, dieting, and obsession with numbers was calling my name. "Come back to the life of calorie count-ing, scale watching, and point counting," my inner voice told me. "We will help you; we promise!"

And I did go back to my old habits. I started looking for ways to track my caloric and carbohydrate intake. I began fasting and juicing, looking for something—anything—that would help me return to my pre-pregnancy weight. I started to limit taking pictures of myself, not wanting my postpartum bump or double chin to ruin a picture with my children. I continued checking my weight on the scale and allowing it to derail days, weeks, and months of happiness. There were times I felt like my entire life was spinning out of control because I wasn't thin enough, which in turn made me feel I wasn't good enough as a mother and a human being.

It took months, but eventually I decided I had enough! You see, I'm a mum of four. That's *four* children who need my time, attention and love! My life of self-loathing immediately postpartum required me to spend so much mental energy counting, tracking, planning, weighing and more. I would plan out my "new diet" and create my new set of rules, which always began on a Monday. I would begin operation weight loss and stay "on track" for a few days, but eventually slip up, call myself out, remind myself of how useless I was, shame my lack of willpower, and binge. Plan, "fail," binge, repeat. And all of that mental real estate that kept the cycle going? It meant *less* of my attention and focus was on my family—and don't get me started on the lack of self-care. The attention I was putting into hating myself could have easily been replaced by joyful moments with my baby and three older children. My negative postpartum body issues were taking over my life, and the rules of dieting and restriction were creating more harm than good!

This past year, I've been learning that there's so much more to life than chasing a body type. I'm learning loads about intuitive eating and body positivity, and what it means to really feel connected to my body! I've also learned that being thin does *not* need to be a major life goal at any time in life. Ignoring my body's hunger cues is not self-care. Being fat, plump, or overweight is okay. My worth is not solely based on my appearance. I'm worthy of love, freedom with food, and success no matter my body shape. I'm an excellent mum and my weight has nothing to do with that. I don't need to "get my body back," as I never lost it to begin with. I'm also not required to hide all of the visible signs of pregnancy. The big lie—this idea of "bouncing back" postpartum—is sold to vulnerable new moms by multi-billion-dollar industries and guess what? This mama doesn't bite. I now recognize my strength. It has always been here, and it has helped me grow, birth, and feed four babies.

I haven't weighed myself in over six months, which initially felt strange and frightening. I no longer buy clothes that are snug or one size too small, hoping they will motivate me to lose weight. I simply purchase the size that is most comfortable; the number on the tag is irrelevant. I don't punish myself if I eat beyond feeling full—I simply own it and move on. I choose exercise that I *enjoy* versus what's going to burn the most calories. I don't track my distance or calories burned. I don't exercise to earn a meal or as punishment for something "bad" I have eaten previously. I start each day new and don't carry any negative feelings with me that might have popped up yesterday. Instead of eating and moving with *the goal* of weight loss, I'm making healthier choices because they feel good inside and out.

Instead of saying, "I hate (or need to change) my body so I'm going to improve it with a diet, detox, etc.," I choose to say, "I love and re-spect my body, so I'm going to listen to it and make choices that support health!" I still eat cake sometimes; I still feel lazy some days, and there are days when I overeat. But you know what? The freedom and peace I have found with body positivity and self-love is such a beautiful place to be!

To my plump postpartum body...I love you and thank you for bringing me this far. My days of hating you and disrespecting you in an effort to change you are over.

- Michelle Mayefske

Postpartum Nest

I truly believe that my ultra-positive and empowering third birth is responsible for my peaceful and powerful postpartum experience with my third child.

With my first two children I felt isolated, disconnected, and generally run ragged. I felt like there wasn't enough of me to go around and every day was in survival mode.

It caught me by surprise how different my third postpartum experience was, and why it was so positive and peaceful. With two other children in the house it really didn't make sense.

I took six years between our second and third children so that my husband and I could catch our breath from having two kids under two years. We had the opportunity to move across the country and all over the place with our kids, build up our businesses, and rebuild ourselves and our marriage during that time.

When we made our first move from Alaska to Florida, we decided to bring only one suitcase per person and live in a furnished home so that we could just get out there and start pursuing my husband's business endeavors. What we accidentally found was a super-simplified life and home that allowed us an easy place to retreat at the end of our days, and truly reconnect and restore ourselves. I think that finding this simplified home life is what made postpartum with my third child so easy.

With my first two children, I was drowning in all of the stuff at home—if you're a mom, you know that it's one or all of the following—like laundry, dishes and toys. Not only was I trying to keep up with the demands of two kids under two, breastfeeding, working, bills, hormonal swings and shifts from all of that and being a young mother, but my home was just another source of burden and frustration for me.

I went out into the world, worked hard, tried to keep up with pumping, was away from my babies while I was working, and then came home to feeling like an absolute failure because I had no time and energy to give my kids *and* my home. Home felt like more work, not a place for me to connect with my family like I wanted to.

When we were finally ready for baby number three to come into the world, we recreated our home space to be intentional and a place that served us. We were still a nomadic family and had just moved to a new state when I found out I was pregnant, and did not have an in-person support system. But because we had learned to create such an intentional atmosphere at home, I knew my postpartum experience would be better.

In addition to having a home that served us—and not one that I felt like a victim to—I had a very transformational birth with my daughter. I had no interventions and was in complete control, able to birth by my intuition. I really feel that helped my body and spirit stay connected and create a stable postpartum. With my first two births, I was given all kinds of medications and interventions that altered my physiology after birth. While I love and appreciate modern medicine's ability to help when needed, I can look back and know that with my first two that those things weren't needed, and my physical health would have been easier to balance after birth without those interventions.

After I had my daughter, I remember coming home and having my two older kids and a newborn baby to care for while my husband was at work. I wanted as much as I possibly could to just stay home and hold her, nurse her, and bond with her during those first weeks and months—without all the excess distractions and work of the home. Not having an in-person support system, this was especially important to me.

It worked out just as I had planned. The toys and laundry from the big kids were massively downsized and simplified and easy to maintain, and I had done the work to teach them how to help me with those tasks.

I communicated with my husband about meals and groceries, and let him know when I needed him to fill in the gaps from grocery shopping or dinners that I wasn't able to get to that week.

I was very focused on the bare minimum for the home so that I could focus my time and energy on building that relationship with my new baby, but also maintaining the relationship with my older kids and husband.

I felt completely at peace in our home that served its purpose for us. My family knew that it was going to be a season of quiet and solitude at home. Many movie nights and game nights in, not going out and doing a lot of excessive errands or trips. On the weekends, my husband took the older kids out for a hike, or to a movie or arcade while the baby and I stayed home so that everyone's needs were met—and wants too.

It made me realize how important it is to make the stuff in our life and home work *for* us and not against us. If we didn't have that experience of ditching all of our material possessions, I believe I still would have been as overwhelmed with postpartum life as I was with my first two children.

I do know that I had the benefit of experience on my side as number three came to the world, and the benefit of having older kids who were more self-sufficient as far their daily demands.

I also experienced many of the same hormonal and physiological changes and swings that come at about six weeks, three months, six months, etc., and remember having days (even with my third) where I cried for no reason and just felt pretty glum. But it wasn't amplified because the rest of my life felt supported.

This was proof to me that yes, as mothers in the postpartum phase there are changes outside of our control that happen within our bodies and minds. We can, however, minimize those experiences by giving ourselves the space to process it all with minimal distractions and obligations.

My hope in sharing this story is to help postpartum mothers realize this is true for themselves too. That yes, the physical and physiologic changes we experience do impact us and can make us feel less than ideal, but those things do not define us as mothers. We can take steps to be proactive in preventing them from getting too intense because the circumstances of our postpartum phase matter, too, and can have just as much—if not more—of a negative impact on our postpartum journeys.

- Krista Lockwood

The Good Belly

Mere days after delivering twins via cesarean, I was in awe of my body and at the same time disgusted by it. After I arrived home, I caught my reflection in the bedroom mirror and stopped to assess the unfamiliar woman in front of me. I stood in silence, hot tears rolling down my cheeks, staring at the extensive skin now hanging from my torso. I was completely shocked by the fresh red lines shredding my flesh, hanging in front of me the remains of my pregnant belly.

My husband caught me in that moment and I quickly covered up. "What's wrong?" He asked. "I am so hideous now," I sobbed. He calmly crossed the room toward me and asked me to uncover my new belly. I reluctantly showed him the horror beneath my clenched hands.

He cupped my most vulnerable body part in his hands and spoke with a surprisingly tender voice for his typically stoic demeanor, "How could you ever think this isn't beautiful? This body gave our babies life and brought them safely into this world."

Those two sentences unlocked a truth inside of me that I had not recognized before. The permanent stripes emblazoned across the surface of my middle represent so much more than my rank in motherhood. They tell my body story. They tell the outside world about my inner strength; that I am a survivor and I will not accept defeat. I brought life into this world despite many obstacles to my own health. Before giving birth, I endured five months of modified bed rest at home. After birth, I needed a full year of physical therapy to untwist my bones and regain my physical strength.

My newly-padded midsection was the result of growing two human beings inside me at the same time. This overly-stretched covering was the protective layer between my growing babies and the elements of our world. My expanding body fought hard against pregnancy complications and the fear of losing another child.

Three years before my daughters made their feisty entrance into the world, another child occupied that same space. A child I had only dreamed of. A child I expected and planned for—and a child I would never meet. Before the arrival of my twins, my body healed from miscarriage. But I couldn't stop thinking about the child that should have been here with us, even now staring at my precious, tiny infants. I felt like a failure. But this belly was good to me this time. It gave me a safe space to create and nurture two humans at once.

As my husband and I stood together without a word between us, we gazed at our sleeping newborns only a few feet away. I looked at them and back at my body and I made the connection: This was all for them. There is a saying, "Scars are like tattoos but with better stories." The scars that now stretch across my good belly not only tell my story, but they illustrate how expansive my love is for my family.

- Roxanne Ferber

The Chasm

Suddenly, and without warning
I found myself in a dark chasm,
deeper and further from the light than I have ever felt.

On every wall was a mirror
that reflected some false truth about myself,
and somehow all of my protective amulets,
my cloaks of wisdom,
my jewels of dignity
could not penetrate the illusions.

I lay sleepless, naked and lost,
overcome by the fear that my newfound predicament would never
end,
however abruptly it had arrived.
All my knowing was swallowed by the heavy weight of shame
I felt at finding myself in this place.

Me—the calm presence,
the grounded, graceful one,
the wise priestess,

the midwife who guides others through labyrinths of treacherous terrain.

Here I was lost in a sea of doubt and fear

and deep, deep sadness.

Would I rise from this descent?

from this abyss of unknown and disregarded

pieces of my soul?

Who was I, if not who I thought I was?

Where was my faith? My ground? My truth?

If none of my tools were working,

or if I simply could not access them,

how would I find a way back to my essence?

Two nights passed, and on the third night I found myself at the gate of desperation.

Here I left behind my necklace of oils and herbs and exchanged it for a chemical elixir

that would guarantee me respite from this nightmare, if only temporarily.

My spirit was weary so I received it gratefully, drinking it in like a thirsty desert traveler.

I was granted several hours of my most coveted medicine—sleep.

Though thankful for the oasis of dreams, I awoke in a daze, quickly realizing that my nightmare was my waking life.

I had not moved from the chasm of mirrors reflecting back the matrix of personal lies...

I'm not enough.

I'm not safe.

I'm alone.

I'm crazy.

I'm a burden.

I was still lost, just a bit more rested.

Panic returned.

How long would this go on?

Where were my children?

How could I care for them from here?

What was the meaning of this labyrinth?

I had passed through the gates of overwhelm, guilt, shame, fear, and sadness so deep it felt impenetrable.

On my descent, I had found my essence again and again after traversing these gates.

But I had never before passed through the Gate of Holy Terror—
not to this degree.

I felt trapped by the never-ending responsibility to love, guide, protect, teach, provide, and nurture

these three babes whom I now carried on my back.

The walls of the chasm were steep, and I wondered how I would
make my ascent when my body

ached with fatigue and depletion.

Yes, the anxiety had lifted.

I had passed through the gate.

But the journey was still long and now I just felt empty—

knowing the work ahead and carrying the weight of depletion,

the shame of having been lost,

the guilt of knowing how much worse it could be and was for so
many other mothers,

the humility of losing touch with my own essence,

of discovering that my own tools and wisdom were not deep
enough to hold me...up until now.

And finally, through a deep dive of faith,

Through expanding, opening, and trusting

that I could find my way—

that the nightmare was purposeful,

and my passage through the chasm of false selves

was all in service to the deepening of my own

chrysalis and ultimately to my emergence as a Motherfly!

- Corina Fitch

Finding Joy After Abuse

After months of planning and preparing my body for a natural childbirth, my body failed me and I ended up in the hospital for an emergency c-section.

I was heartbroken, angry, devastated...and now in a massive, surgery-induced fog. Not at all how I wanted to feel as a new mom. And yet, my daughter was completely perfect and healthy, which was the most important thing.

I had thought about and planned for every angle—including c-section if absolutely necessary. I just never thought it would happen, and how that would shake me to my very core.

Luckily, I surrounded myself from the beginning with such incredible people and caregivers who helped me through all of it, and even grieved with me as they were also shocked by the direction my body took us.

A very important thing we all knew from the moment I found out I was pregnant was that I would most likely be on my own, as my boyfriend at the time had relapsed again. Within weeks of finding out I was pregnant, he was arrested and sent to rehab.

I chose my midwife for a handful of reasons, but mainly because I felt safe with her and she had been in a situation very similar to my own when delivering her daughter years ago. So she knew all the care I could possibly need very well.

Because of the stress and the fear from this bad, limping relationship, I was in supermom mode from the beginning in an obsessive way. I was in tip-top shape throughout my pregnancy. My hypervigilance was my saving grace on my road to recovering from birth.

Yes, I did stay in that relationship for awhile for two reasons. There was once a lot of love there. And, should it end, I knew that one day I would need to explain to my child why I left her father. I needed to be able to say that I did everything in my power to help him and keep us together, and mean it.

And here is the even harder truth about abusive relationships: it's not all abusive or bad. It is extremely hard to leave someone who is loving and caring the majority of the time. I had to leave when I was truly ready and had the strength to be on my "own." I was not lacking support; I was lacking my own internal strength.

It is important to know this because the bad part showed up and kick-started my contractions. It also stopped my laboring completely when he arrived to the birthing center while high, and had to be removed from the premises. His behavior, choices, disease, etc. had physical impacts on me.

While I was in the hospital and in the weeks to follow, my midwife and doulas checked in me and my baby girl several times. And during one of those visits, she told me something that would forever change the way I viewed my body.

My body did exactly what it was supposed to do when faced with real threats. There was a not a physical reason why I couldn't fully give birth—my body just knew she was safer inside the womb than in the outside world. It's something that my doula also saw in other women who were in bad relationships.

I carried this information with me throughout my recovery and the early months with my daughter. I started listening to my body more. Instead of ignoring my body to get something done, I would honor it and prioritize what needed to be done to care for my daughter.

Just like I was hypervigilant during pregnancy, I stayed hypervigilant during postpartum. I did anything and everything suggested to stay healthy, in every sense of the word.

This included: breastfeeding, eating for baby (diaper rash nutrition was so hard, but worth it!), walking outside, therapy, La Leche League, mommy friends, asking for help from family, not having a spotless home, so on and so forth. Doing all of this helped me feel like I had a little bit of control in my life that was otherwise spiraling in some way.

But one of the number one thing I did for myself was remove a huge, daily anxiety-inducer—Facebook.

My daughter's dad popped in and out of our lives for the first year. Even on those good days with him, the social media comparison and jealousy were insurmountable for me. I just couldn't handle it; I became overwhelmed with grief for myself and my daughter.

The Daddy-Daughter Dance pictures did me in. As much as I wanted to feel joy for other people and acquaintances in my life, I just didn't have the capability at the time. So, I disabled my account. I didn't have one again for a couple of years, until I needed it for work. This choice really helped me stay focused on my journey with my daughter and grow our bond.

In some ways, the odds were definitely not stacked in my favor. But regardless of anyone's situation, there are so many challenges during postpartum and learning to care for this tiny being. It took being honest with myself and my support network to find what worked best for me and my daughter.

For me, the challenge was honoring and listening to my body, giving myself space and grace to grieve the birth and relationship that I didn't have, and removing the seemingly innocent things that were causing me distress. Because I did that, we found the joy in our journey!

- Anonymous

Anchors in the Storm

I felt on top of the world. The moment my son was born, I felt like I could run a marathon, jump through the roof, and eat all the sushi! I was in the zone, so to speak, trying to be my own advocate as the circumstances of my son's birth called for some different measures. My second son was born in the car on the way to the hospital, as I squatted facing backwards in the front passenger seat, with my two-year-old in the backseat watching as the postpartum period officially began. Once my son was born, the pain was immediately relieved, and I felt absolutely powerful. Because I was in the car, I could only keep squatting over the mixture of blood, vaginal fluids, and waters on the seat, while holding my seconds-old son, smelling his hair and smearing in the vernix all over his fresh skin.

I just wanted to go home. I knew we wouldn't make it to the hospital on time, and as we were leaving, I'd jokingly said that he would be born in the car. But we went anyway, to my dismay. It was clearly too close. And this is where it all began—my postpartum story.

Searching for clarification on what postpartum means, the first thing that comes up in search engines is postpartum depression. Not just "the time following childbirth," but a full peer-reviewed article on the fact that postpartum depression occurs in many women soon after giving birth. While most new moms experience postpartum "baby blues" after childbirth, many also fall much further than they ever imagined. Why are there so many scary articles about postpartum out there, and not the encouraging ones that share how much of a gift it is? If there was more camaraderie, information, and support for what to expect; or advice from those you love and entrust your care to (for both the new baby and other children), then my postpartum experience might have been night and day compared to what actually happened.

When the EMTs showed up in the back of the grocery store parking lot in small-town east Texas, I should have felt that all would have been well. But I wasn't so sure, and for good reason. My son was born 40 minutes into a one-hour drive to the hospital, and I wasn't even confident in giving birth there seeing as I started having prenatal care so late in the pregnancy due to insurance discrepancies (that we're still dealing with a year and a half later). My first minutes postpartum were kind of an out-of-body experience, holding my fresh son while begging to just turn around and go home or straight to our family nurse practitioner an hour away...and instead being greeted by an ambulance. Yet the EMTs were so incredibly kind, cutting the cord six inches from baby after it turned white once baby received the last one third of his blood. They were careful not to look at me, and surrounded me with towels to walk the few yards from the car to the ambulance, in the middle of the morning on an ordinary Sunday in a grocery parking lot with onlookers peering. How vulnerable, right?

As I settled into the ambulance, the medics were making their report notes and saying that "this has never happened to them" while I was just sitting there watching my baby boy do his newborn thing. They were so calm and attentive to my son and I, giving baby a "space blanket" to stay warm; not being embarrassed when I started to nurse him with a blanket around us; and asking questions about how I felt, the timeline of events, where the hospital was, and all of that. I jokingly said I was relieved and empowered to do it all on my own in my own way, albeit in the car, and they agreed, "That's one way to do it." The calm 20-minute drive to the hospital in the back of the ambulance was some of the only peace I had postpartum.

Once we made it to the hospital, they didn't know what to do with us. I completed the initial paperwork just a month earlier because our birth plans were up in the air for a while. As I was learning about the birth process and what I wanted, I just couldn't make a decision, so I chose to be as informed as possible and prepared to go on my own if need be. Yet our information was in the system, and eventually they put us in a room usually reserved for labor. Once in the room, it was time for the placenta to be delivered, and immediately all the pain was gone. I was really excited to see my placenta and in awe of what this organ, unique to pregnancy, does and supports.

I wanted to make my own placenta pills and was prepared to do it at home, so I asked to keep it and the nurses put it in a container. But by the time we left the room a couple hours later, they would not let me take it because it wasn't cooled over ice. Nobody brought ice when I asked because they were in a rush to see us, and they didn't let us out of the room to get ice and a bucket at a machine down the hall. I knew the placenta would have been fine sitting out just another 15 minutes until we could get to the mother-baby floor, where they had an ice machine and bags for containing it, but that wasn't acceptable for protocol. That was the second time my wishes weren't taken seriously.

Family arrived from out of town, and we made our way to a room on the mother-baby unit. The postpartum rooms at this hospital were very nice, but all I really wanted was to be home. I didn't even deliver our baby at the hospital, and I felt great, so what reason did we have to be there? Time in the hospital would add so many unnecessary bills, and they don't even know what to do with us! But we stayed, after our family's and the staff's reassurance. I was finally able to eat in the afternoon—I barely ate all morning while in labor, then arrived to the hospital after lunchtime and was waiting in limbo for a bit...I was so incredibly hungry! And then as I was trying to eat, all the post-birth protocol had to happen. An IV inserted just in case it was needed, although I already had the baby in my arms. Different nurses, doctors, and staff coming in to check on us. Extra personnel stopping in to see the "car baby" they heard about, because the whole floor was abuzz. All the interruptions happened at once, but I did have my perfect, whole baby boy, and physically I felt great and finally had some food.

Then I rested and bonded with baby. Finally the routine rounds of vitals were done, and we had some quiet time in our room without interruption so we could rest. The hospital food was surprisingly good, the nurses were kind, and the pediatrician was extremely laid-back and pro-parents' choice. He gave us the okay to leave the next morning once he made his rounds; it was a relief to me to have such a short stay. My husband went back to the house to get us clothes and such for the overnight stay, since I didn't have a bag packed yet.

Overnight there were more interruptions for checking vitals, and of course nursing baby, changing baby, and resting as I could. Then sometime past midnight, just as we finally went to sleep, the fire alarms went off and we were rushed into the hallway for a drill. It took some time to get us all settled again after that, so we barely slept that night. The entire stay was full of slight inconveniences that affected how I experienced postpartum and the days to come.

Morning came, and after taking newborn and family pictures, getting vitals checked, and a brief miscommunication about out-processing procedures that caused me mental anguish and tears of frustration, we were cleared to leave. Postpartum is such a vulnerable time, and even though my wishes, backed by provoking scientific research and biblical knowledge, were ultimately honored, it was a difficult conversation. So we went home, and my mom stayed with us a few days to help postpartum.

Back at home, I got into gear with all of my initial preparations: homemade rice heating pads, nipple cream, and making padsicles for comfort; pumping for extra milk storage and washable nursing pads; initiating belly binding with homemade paste and a beautiful blue and purple fabric; and using a curved peri bottle filled with witch hazel, lavender, aloe, and warm water for extra relief, long with an herbal perennial spray. Even though many never knew about it, I did a lot of preparation during pregnancy for the birth and postpartum period, as I wanted to enjoy it and honor it.

I wanted to understand what was going on with my body, not just put up with it. Knowledge is power, after all, and despite the circumstances I felt empowered in birth because of this knowledge. And having these items ready postpartum—especially the padsicles—made it better. I can barely describe the relief of pulling the first one out of the freezer! Anyone that has birthed a child knows what I'm talking about.

A few days later we took our son to our family nurse practitioner, who is our primary care provider and also a lactation consultant—we seriously won the lottery with her! The visit was focused primarily on making sure baby was gaining weight and we were doing well. And all was mostly well.

In the next few days, friends brought casseroles and meals for the week and we rested into life with a newborn and toddler. Baby loved his mamaRoo swing, which fit perfectly in the corner of the boys' room in our tiny house; and big brother loved taking his toys and setting them by baby's feet. The routine of nursing, changing, rocking, light rest, and taking care of an older sibling began.

Aside from this, my postpartum time did take a somewhat sour turn. While being very prepared, I was also fairly misunderstood, because I chose to do things differently than with my first. While being informed and advocating for yourself is a great thing, it can also appear different to others who don't know. Some of these decisions were ridiculed by those close to me, which left me feeling isolated and unable to talk to anyone. Even the series of events that led us to being in the car during the birth made me uncomfortable to think about, as I feel it could have been avoided. Reflecting on what happened surrounding labor and birth is what got me down during postpartum, and I should have known better. But I didn't.

Postpartum typically describes the critical first six weeks after birth up to six months later. So considering that period, the remainder of my postpartum time didn't go as well as I wanted and hoped. With all the misunderstandings came more miscommunication. Writing out the birth story and how I felt helped so much, but it still continued.

My brother and sister-in-law had their first baby exactly two weeks after mine, so there were many family visits planned for the future. And just two months later was the first time we all got together, on one side of the family. Things were tense with our current situation and miscommunication surrounding the birth and postpartum, and I felt so misunderstood.

Looking back at pictures, I could see it—I was barely there. It was good to be away with a change of scenery, taking the kids to the zoo and exploring a small town in another state, but I was still reeling with what happened during my baby's birth, and the way I was spoken to and treated by everyone in the room right afterward based on my preferences. I know ultimately that birth is out of our control, and I can't change the past. But the way I felt and was misunderstood—because my wishes and expectations surrounding my birth and the time wasn't taken seriously—still plagued me. I felt all alone without that village of support I so desperately wanted, because I had it in some ways but was missing it in others. When our expectations don't meet reality, however noble or honorable they may be, it can cause our minds to do crazy things. Add to that postpartum hormones and, well...

I spiraled. We lost it. And soon after that trip, I was met with the plagued thoughts again, and things almost took a turn for worse. I was so close, standing at the edge of our pond. But I had a toddler and a newborn, and that's when the misunderstandings became so great that I was told to take an unwelcome break. I went away with the kids to stay with family, because it was best for me to have some peace and rest, and for everyone to regroup. I ended up being away for two weeks, when baby was between two and three months old. The time still messed with me, because although needed, it was all unwelcome. I felt so pitiful, begging to be somewhere else and not wanting to deal with how our family dynamics had changed. But I was still trying to be intentional and in the moment with my two boys, as I was so prepared before the baby was born. I didn't see that time away as a gift, as I should have; maybe if I had, it would have been different. So when I went home, I spiraled again when another discrepancy came about. I just couldn't get ahold of myself and I still felt so alone in everything, even though the circumstances weren't all my fault. The household was asleep; I called a hotline and then I went to bed.

I jumped into nutrition and prayer, and finding a new way to relate to God in all this experience. I did counseling and writing, too. Journaling has power, and putting to pen the thoughts in your mind is...eye opening. It helps you improve clarity, see patterns, and put words to what you are feeling. I slowly tried to find myself again as everything seemed to be unravelling around me. And honestly, life still is a mess— nothing will ever be perfect as we think it should be—but a year and a half later, I finally feel like I'm out of that postpartum fog. I'm feeling more myself, free to be me, and not stuck in that place due to circumstance and what others said or did to me. I'm not letting that get to me and mix with the crazy hormones which led to the spiral. And yes, it's taken that long.

I'll end with this: all the preparation in the world for your ideal birth will not quite prepare you for what happens in birth and how you will feel, let alone your experiences immediately postpartum. All the teas, belly wraps, herbs and oils, books, padsicles, and lactation cookies in the world wouldn't have prepared me for what my mind and body went through in those months postpartum—or the misunderstandings in those first few days. But there is a silver lining, in that no matter the type of experience you have, writing your story has power; nourishing your body with ancient wisdom aides in so many facets; counseling is a strength for your hard moments; and prayer is your anchor in the storm to keep you grounded in faith as you walk through this time.

- Katherine Newsom

Becoming a Mother of Two

No. No this can't be. I'm not ready!

And yet, the digital word "pregnant" stared back at me from the stick in my shaking hand.

A strange mix of shock, happiness, fear, and gratitude swept over me.

We both knew we wanted a second child. But not now.

Not so soon.

You see, I had milestones to accomplish before trying for a second.

I wanted to get my pre-baby body back. I wanted to find a way out of my 9-5 job so that I could finally, happily remain at home to care for my little ones. And our apartment! I wanted to move out of here and into a nice house with a yard. How were we to expand our family in these close quarters?

I didn't know how I was going to do this. Be pregnant again. Be pregnant and still care for my one-year-old. Work full time. Breastfeed. Pump. Figure out the cost of daycare for two. Sleepless nights. The actual labor and delivery! All at once, images of my new life ahead bombarded my brain and anxiety kicked in.

Being the perfectionist that I am, I wanted a plan for baby number two. I wanted to be in control and ahead of the situation. But now, as the reality of my surprise pregnancy sank in, deep down festered a fear that I felt so guilty to even acknowledge existed.

The logistics of pregnancy I knew I could handle. Inconvenient and difficult? Yes. But I would face them and survive. Put one foot in front of the other. Focus on one moment at a time, one day at a time.

No. There was another, deeper fear pulling at me.

I didn't know how I was going to adjust from one child to two— how I could possibly love the second as much and as completely as the first.

Because my first was everything to me. Through her, I discovered a whole new level of love that I could never before imagine, understand, or empathize with. Through her, I was given the gift of a Mother's Love.

So now, with a second baby on the way, what would happen with this love? Would it be split, transformed, changed? I didn't understand, and I was afraid. Afraid of not feeling the same level of love towards my second as I did the first. Or, maybe even worse, of experiencing a shift of that love to my new baby and inevitably forgetting how strongly I felt towards my first.

I didn't know how this love would come to be...but I chose to believe that it would.

As the months progressed, I caught glimpses of that love through the actions of my now almost two-year-old. Still too young to really grasp the concept of a human baby, she nonetheless paid special attention to my ever-growing bump.

She wrapped her arms around it and rested her head against it. Repeated "baby" with a smile. And my heart stirred with gratitude and care for both little souls entrusted to me.

My due date came...and went.

I remember sitting in a recliner chair one summer afternoon. My daughter had fallen asleep in my arms, awkwardly positioned with my 40-plus-weeks bump. I remember feeling so hot and uncomfortable. But there was no way I would move her.

These fleeting moments, I knew, were the last of an era. An era of her being my one and only. My baby girl. And as I sat there quietly in that lazy afternoon, tears streamed down my face as I simultaneously mourned and celebrated this transition.

Finally, the day arrived. Our family of three became four.

Here she finally was. Pink and wrinkly; soft and small and perfect. Mother's Love, personified.

With her in my arms, all my motherly instincts increased tenfold from pregnancy. I felt an immediate fierce protectiveness. An inexplicable level of love, adoration, obsession that could only be birthed alongside my baby herself.

Those little fingers that curl around your own, those dark eyes that gaze at you, the nose and mouth that instinctively and single-mindedly seek you out for warmth, safety, and nourishment. I was her everything.

What was I so concerned about before? This little life was a true miracle that I was privileged to raise and call my own. I could not imagine our family without her.

So when my first born entered the hospital room, my fears were dismissed. She ran up to the bed where I sat cradling her baby sister, and looked at her with such excitement that I knew it would be okay. Because her face and her presence also filled me with complete joy.

"Baby?" she asked, a smile on her face. Then she bent down and kissed her baby sister on the head.

I truly recognized then what power love has. It is bigger than what my mind can wrap around—what others try to explain it as. My love for one does not exceed what I feel for the other. The birth of my second does not take away from the joy I felt at the birth of my first. Instead, the love is compounded, elevated, magnified.

It is too great for me to analyze or comprehend. But I know it is there, as I faithfully believed it would be.

Now, months later, life is chaotic, messy, loud, and at times frustrating, stressful, and hilarious. But always beautiful.

I savor the moments I get to spend alone with my baby girl, our newest addition. Relishing in the baby snuggles and cuddles. And I also treasure the moments alone that I make for my first born. She is now a leader. A trail-blazer, a protector for her little sister.

Their smiles towards one another are priceless. Any plan I could have fashioned, well, I no longer want it. Because there is no perfect time, no ideal situation that could have prepared me for the love and appreciation I feel for both my girls.

Is my body where I want it to be? Not yet. Are we still in an apartment? Yes. But I'm learning it doesn't really matter where we live, or what my work situation is like. I have my daughters, my family, and through them life is so special. So complete.

For now, I am enjoying this new era because I know it is fleeting. And I want to be able to look back on this time, and know that I embraced the messy, the imperfect. We will figure out the rest, the logistics, one moment at a time. One day at a time.

- Kimberly Black

The Raw Edges of Postpartum

The glass has shattered.

Only the "glass" I'm referring to happens to be the very body I inhabit. Physically, this vessel isn't the same. Emotionally, it's unrecognizable.

Having a baby isn't supposed to be this hard, right? I had the most gorgeous home birth. My sweet baby is healthy. Yet, I feel like my life has ended. Everything has changed, and I don't recognize any of it.

I see the pieces of glass shattered on the floor. I could never be put together again, but I also have no idea how to sweep up the mess.

For the rest of my postpartum experience, I wrestled my way back to what I knew as reality—to a place that felt familiar and whole. My journey involved thorough research and massively heavy tears. It wasn't that I needed to heal from the birth itself, but there was something deep within me that felt *wrong*. Unsurprisingly, I wasn't the only woman who felt this way. Postpartum depression and anxiety and are so familiar to our society that they define the very word "postpartum." These feelings I shared with so many others were a part of a collective societal group of struggling mothers that, unfortunately seems to be growing exponentially.

As "normal" as my symptoms were, the professionals have little to no understanding why women feel this way postpartum. It became clear that medical science deemed it a hormonal problem, blaming my body's inability to fully recover from the most ancient of women's rites: giving birth. As unfair and unjust as it sounds, I refused to believe such a thing.

I kept digging. Slowly, I began to unravel these elemental truths of postpartum. As foreign as they were in my holistic approach to living, their ideas spoke to me deeply and I stitched each finding into a quilt of hope; wrapping my unrecognizable body in its optimism as tight as possible.

It seemed that many of these truths were long lost traditions of our women. We once held onto the belief that postpartum was a sacred time of healing and rejuvenation, and bathed each new mother in nourishing meals, optimal rest, and the most luxurious 40 days post-birth as possible.

These ancient truths and cultural traditions are unknown to our modern ways of living. The new societal belief is that we as women should "bounce back" after having a baby; that if baby is healthy then we should be happy; and that our tendency toward postpartum depression and anxiety are a normal part of being a mother. In other places across the world, however, where giving birth is considered a rite of passage and mothers are given ample time to heal their bodies, rates of postpartum depression and anxiety are almost non-existent.

Personally, I lost out on this intense time of healing. In my guilt for not wanting to take up anyone else's time, I did my best to get back to a *normal* routine quickly. I certainly didn't want to burden anyone with my need to heal, and I spent my days doing everything *but* resting. The sacrifice of this short stretch of time destroyed my health, my hormones, and made my relationship with my son the most guilt-ridden phase of my life. I couldn't reverse time and try again. But I could start over.

My journey began by accepting the loss of who I once was, because carrying a baby within your body changes who you are in a fundamental way. Creating another human being changes a mother at a cellular level, meaning that every cell in my body was forever changed by the child I carried within me. I would never be the same person.

Naptime and bedtime became critical moments of healing. After mourning my previous life and accepting that I was a new woman, I needed to discover who that woman was. Journaling, painting, meditation, and bodywork were my guidebooks. Piece by piece, the shattered glass began to be picked up.

Like most mothers in modern culture, I didn't experience the age-old deep healing that can accompany birth. Instead, I was offered another way to heal my body and watch the transformation of who I was move from maiden to mother. This very trek meant that I had to endure the difficult and brave; the unseen. Birth has a way of splitting a woman wide open, shedding her layers and exposing her roots, that causes a natural dive inward natural and makes healing customary. Healing after this sacred time period has passed, however, means that a mother must carry a shovel and dig her up her own roots—a process that resembles labor all over again.

Through this rebirth, I was able to pick the pieces of shattered glass off the floor. Piece by piece, I glued them back together, adding pops of color and unique trinkets along the way, until the end result equaled a beautiful stained glass. When I hold it up to the sun, I see a beautiful rainbow shine on my precious son.

Many years later, I went on have more children. Through trembling fingers, I announced my second pregnancy and rode the waves of uncertainty until birth. My daughter came into the world so fast and furious that I was left to birth her with only my husband present. To deliver my own child into the world was the most empowering experience I'd ever encountered at the time.

It was as if the challenges of pregnancy and labor—or my past struggles with postpartum depression and anxiety—had never existed. I was higher than a kite, soaking up every ounce of my newborn's life and completely in awe of my own power to bring her earthside.

My inner strength and pride for such accomplishment made me feel like I could do anything. And despite my knowledge of all things postpartum, I took this feeling to mean that I could and, therefore, I did. I felt like my body was giving me permission but in reality, it was healing slowly and gently as it should.

It wasn't long before I crashed, and I finally realized that the grace of healing gently wasn't a sign that I could do more. Within months, my world came to an abrupt halt. But it wasn't that I just woke up one day feeling miserable. It was the realization that my body had given me all the signs that it was hurting and I failed to see them until the pain became unbearable. Once again, I had failed my body.

I developed what appeared to be a tumor in my stomach. MRIs and many appointments later, it was discovered that my "tumor" was simply scar tissue left over from a long-ago surgery. But in the process of investigating this scare, I also found out that I had ulcerative colitis. My intestines felt as if they were being stabbed by a million knives all at once. I became rageful and angry at myself, my family, and my situation. I hated the world for bringing me another child my body couldn't raise. And I'd spend countless hours crying over it on the toilet, which held my pain and blood from my new disease.

Another beautiful baby girl came into my life. Not yet healed from the second, we found out we were pregnant again. I cried in disbelief. My body was so broken, how could I bring another baby into the world? Would this pregnancy be safe? Prenatal depression struck hard and my struggle with my body continued to ebb and flow.

She came into this world as healthy as her siblings. And through it all, I felt confident in my postpartum. I knew what to expect, how to take it slow, how important nutrition was, and sought help from my husband while making sure he knew how much sleep and support I would need.

But alas, my meal train fell through. My husband had to return to work. My intestines felt the pains of my disease. My oldest daughter become constantly ill through undiagnosed asthma. And I fell apart.

This time, however, I landed face first into postpartum bipolar. My lows had me in the closet, crying on the floor and begging God to stop this disaster. Wondering why I was given children. Wondering how long I was going to suffer. And the next day, I would be so full of energy that I packed up the kids for a hike across a valley in the mountains, singing children's songs and dancing to their giggles, only to be on the closet floor again the following day.

It was through my highs that I realized what I was experiencing. I didn't want to believe it, and several conversations with my healthcare provider had me scared out of my mind. I had three kids to care for, including an infant. Letting this continue wasn't an option.

I made the choice to get better immediately. My priority in life shifted to focus only on my health and everything that served me. I didn't feel selfish this time, as I knew that by caring for myself deeply in this way I would be simultaneously caring for my family. This simple shift in thinking fueled my need to get better. I wasn't going to repeat what happened after my first and second babies. And I'd be damned I'd let it be worse.

I used my high periods to execute the knowledge I had about postpartum. I followed it with more research. Cooked a weeks' worth of healing postpartum meals in a day. Bought more sitz bath blends, better vitamins, tincture, teas, essential oils...anything I could get my hands on. I told my husband we had to find a way to get me better sleep and make it a priority again to follow through. And I started journaling. I poured my soul into writing down my thoughts and feelings and uncovering my fears, wounds, and traumas. More importantly, I was able to release them.

My low periods still remained for some time. But their intensity began to lighten up. I went from feeling like my heart would explode in the pile of clothes in my closet to softy crying as I strapped my baby to my back for a walk around the block. Within weeks of intensely caring for myself, I realized I was out of it.

But it became so clear to me in those few months of bipolar that my health and well-being should always be a priority (and why weren't they?). Not only did I witness a change in my own health, especially as the months went on and I began healing my autoimmune disease; I also realized that my entire family revolves around the health of the mother. My need for self-care wasn't just to keep my mental health in check, it was also necessary for my children and my husband.

Another few years later, I went on to have another baby girl. The postpartum experience with her was incomparable.

I spent my entire pregnancy going through the inner work of releasing and letting go at another level I had yet to know even existed. I created my own postpartum meals so that I knew I had what I needed. Pelvic floor physical therapy and chiropractic care became my only outings. My husband took off work for two solid months while I healed. My journaling continued on. And I kept reminding myself over and over about how the brain changes; how the hormonal fluctuations were normal and to just support them. I reminded myself how powerful and beautiful and deserving I was. And I lived in that space.

I didn't get out of bed (except for the bathroom or a bath) for an entire week. I didn't put clothes on for nearly two weeks. A walk to my backyard with the sun shining down felt glorious to me. I didn't need much else.

So much of my postpartum experiences were about allowing myself to emerge as new person. To shed the layers of hurt, trauma, drama, and everything in between, so that I could become the mother that my children needed me to be. When I allowed myself to see my own bullshit, where I was standing in my own way, and how my fears perpetuated my sad story, I could release it and let it go.

Over the years being of creating children, my experiences transformed into a passion for postpartum. In working with mothers, I've applied many of the same principles to healing the body, both immediately after birth as well as after the sacred postpartum time has passed. Although the process is different between the time periods, the results are always the same: a mindful mother who feels empowered, strong, and whole.

***

The medical model of care that modern society operates in (as we know it) will not be responsible for changing the health of mothers in postpartum. In reality, the prevalence of this model will the very thing that continues to bring mothers closer to their grave, both in terms of actual physical demise as well as mental and spiritual health

The health and healing of our mothers will be our own doing, brought on by community and valuing self-care. Mothers will create a new societal paradigm when they stand up and declare that their postpartum needs shall be met, and make space for the community to join in. Not a single woman would be left to struggle in the unknown of what postpartum truly is. And not a single mother would be left to pick up her own shattered body.

But first, we must place importance on our own postpartum experiences. Much like the births we spend months planning for, we ought to also use that time to understand and prepare for postpartum. Making room for this pivotal and life-changing time makes a lasting impression, affecting us on every plane.

Although I spent a great deal of time picking up my own shattered glass pieces, I've discovered that most, if not all, of my postpartum woes could have been prevented with the right care. The female body, in all its glory and perfection, isn't emotionally or hormonally flawed—our bodies aren't failing us. It is simply the belief system and inadequate care in which we expose our raw and open postpartum bodies that are the problem.

It is said that birth isn't just about making babies, it's about making mothers too. And every mother deserves to have the sun shine through her beautiful stained glass, making rainbows for the children she bore within.

- Maranda Bower

Postpartum Resources

When a woman feels abundantly supported in postpartum, many exceptional things happen. I create space for mothers to experience deep healing, no matter where she is in the years after birthing a baby.

For a deeper and more thorough understanding of your personal postpartum needs, you can work with me, Maranda Bower, one-on-one. This is specifically for women in the first few years postpartum and are wanting to finally get back into their body and feel good in it, especially when past/current traumas and physical ailments, including postpartum depression/anxiety and autoimmune issue have impacted them

Learn more here: www.SerenityGrows.com

Breastfeeding:

- www.kellymom.com/
- www.breastfeeding.com/
- www.bfmed.org/
- www.drjacknewman.com/
- www.thefeministbreeder.com/
- www.biologicalnurturing.com/
- www.breastfeedingmadesimple.com/

- www.breastfeedingplace.com/
- https://toxnet.nlm.nih.gov/cgi-bin/sis/htmlgen?LACTMED
- www.llli.org
- Supported in Breastfeeding: Stories of Nourishing Wisdom by Maranda Bower
- The Womanly Art Of Breastfeeding by Diane Wiessinger
- The Nursing Mother's Companion by Kathleen Huggins
- Breastfeeding Made Simple: Seven Natural Laws for Nursing Mothers by Nancy Mohrbacher
- Ina May's Guide to Breastfeeding by Ina May Gaskin

Cesarean:

- www.ican-online.org/
- www.vbac.com/
- www.scienceandsensibility.org/page/april-resources/

Exercise:

- www.diastasisrehab.com/
- www.mutusystem.com/
- www.befitmom.com/

Healing Postpartum:

- Maternity Leave: A New Mother's Guide to the First Six Weeks Postpartum by Cheryl Zauderer, PhD, CNM, NPP, IBCLC
- The Mommy Plan: Restoring Your Postpregnancy Body Naturally, Using Women's Traditional Wisdom by Valerie Lynn

Healing Trauma:

- www.birthingfromwithin.com/pages/birth-story-medicine/
- www.sacredhealing.org/
- www.birthintobeing.com/
- www.karenmelton.com/articles/somecauses-of-womb-birth-trauma/

Nourishing Foods:

- www.serenitygrows.com/postpartumnutrition

- www.yogawithkayaresources.com/postpartum-food-list.html/
  www.foodrenegade.com/ayurvedicwisdom-for-post-partum-recovery/
- www.nourishingmeals.com/2009/05/nourishing-new-mom.html/

Mothering Baby:

- www.motheringarts.com/
- www.mothering.com/
- www.parenting.com/article/11important-baby-cues/
- Magical Beginning, Enchanted Lives by Deepak Chopra
- The Fifth Trimester: The Working Mom's Guide to Style, Sanity, and Big Success After Baby by Lauren Smith Brody
- Happiest Baby on the Block by Harvey Karp, MD
- Aromatherapy for Babies and Children by Shirley Price
- Becoming Us: 8 Steps to Grow a Family that Thrives by Elly Taylor
- www.babywearinginternational.org/

Placenta:

- www.findplacentaencapsulation.com/

- www.bellybelly.com.au/birth/placentaencapsulation/

Postpartum Mood Disorders:

- When Postpartum Packs a Punch: Fighting Back and Finding Joy by Kristina Cowan
- Birth of a New Brain: Healing from Postpartum Bipolar Disorder by Dyane Harwood
- A Mother's Climb Out Of Darkness: A Story about Overcoming Postpartum Psychosis by Jennifer Moyer
- Tokens of Affection: Reclaiming Your Marriage After Postpartum Depression by Karen Kleiman
- Postpartum Depression and Anxiety: A Self-Help Guide for Mothers by Pacific Postpartum Support Society
- Dropping the Baby and Other Scary Thoughts by Karen Kleiman and Amy Wenzel
- The Pregnancy and Postpartum Anxiety Workbook by Pamela S. Wiegartz

Postpartum Partner:

- The Postpartum Husband: Practical Solutions for Living with Postpartum Depression by Karen Kleiman

- www.postpartummen.com/
- www.postpartumdads.org/
- www.postpartum.net/family/tips-forpostpartum-dads-and-partners/

Postpartum Sleep:

- www.kellymom.com/parenting/nighttime/cosleeping/
- www.cosleeping.org/
- www.snugglemeorganic.com/cosleeping-bed-sharing-re-sources/
- www.postpartumprogress.com/dealing-postpartum-sleepdep-rivation/